I Know
Things Now

I Know Things Now

Stories by Teenagers 1

Edited by
Carl Koch

Saint Mary's Press
Christian Brothers Publications
Winona, Minnesota

Claudia Rubio, cover artist, Gonzaga Preparatory School, Spokane, WA

The publishing team included Carl Koch, development editor; Laurie Berg Rohda, manuscript editor; Gary J. Boisvert, typesetter; Maurine R. Twait, art director; pre-press, printing, and binding by the graphics division of Saint Mary's Press.

The excerpt on page 36 is from the musical *Into the Woods*, music and lyrics by Stephen Sondheim, book by James Lapine (1987).

The scriptural quotation on page 93 is from the New Revised Standard Version of the Bible. Copyright © 1989 by the Division of Christian Education of the National Council of the Churches of Christ in the United States of America. Used with permission. All rights reserved.

Printed in the United States of America

Printing: 9 8 7 6 5 4 3 2 1

Year: 2004 03 02 01 00 99 98 97 96

ISBN 0-88489-384-7

 Genuine recycled paper with 10% post-consumer waste. Printed with soy-based ink.

Alicia DiBenedetto
Boylan Catholic High School
Rockford, Illinois

Contents

Carl Koch
Editor

Preface

"Once upon a time . . ."

"Did you hear about the time . . . ?"

These phrases immediately attract our attention because human beings love listening to and telling stories. Storytelling is as natural as breathing, and as ancient as the cave dwellers' bragging and miming about the kill of the day around a campfire. We tell stories about the most serious events in our lives, and the most wacky. We love stories for a lot of reasons:

Stories tell us who we are. When we tell other people a story, we reveal a lot about who we are—not only to them, but to ourselves. The poet Robert Frost says this about writing, "For me the initial delight is in the surprise of remembering something I didn't know I knew." In the hurry of life, we may have missed the importance of an event when it happened. Telling the story of the event helps us realize what it really meant—even years later. So when we tell our story, we discover ourselves in new ways.

Stories help us feel less alone. As we listen to and tell stories, we realize that our story is a part of the great human story, that our feelings and experiences—while new and significant to us—are part of the universal human experience. We are not alone. Other people have felt as we do. Our story can affirm other people; their story can help us understand life better.

We encounter God in our stories. Many times when we tell stories, we begin to realize that life is filled with mystery. What we expect to happen does not happen; what does happen is unexpected. And frequently we begin to recognize the mysterious ways God has acted in our life.

We also listen to stories because they provide entertainment, because they are an outlet for our feelings and desires, and because they can make a point in an interesting way.

These Stories by Teenagers

Teenagers enjoy telling their stories as much as anyone. Unfortunately, young women and men have few avenues for sharing their experiences and insights.

Saint Mary's Press has dedicated itself to sharing the Good News with young people. In the process, young people have shared their insights, courage, generosity, kindness, wisdom, patience, justice, and honesty—the Good News—with us.

Two earlier books from Saint Mary's Press attest to just how much faith, hope, and love live in the hearts of young men and women. *Dreams Alive* and *More Dreams Alive* are filled with wonderful prayers and reflections written by teenagers from all over the country. These books demonstrated how much teenagers have to offer.

Given our experience with the two books of prayers and reflections, we at Saint Mary's Press decided to invite teenagers to share their stories. In October 1994, we asked the religion and English department chairpersons of all the Catholic high schools in the United States to invite their students to send their stories to us. To give focus to the stories, the guidelines read: "We would like first-person narratives that relate to this question: What has been your most memorable experience of good coming out of a bad situation, or kindness in the midst of ugliness, or hope in darkness, or growth in the midst of difficulty?"

Students could withhold their names or use their initials, their first name, or their full name. We wanted to ensure that students could be honest in telling their stories. In this book, the names of some of the writers have been withheld because the stories are so honest that they or those they write about should have their privacy protected.

By April 1995, scores of stories had been submitted by high schools from coast to coast, Guam, and the U.S. Virgin Islands. After an initial sorting, I asked six students to help make the final selection: Rachel Dahdal, from Winona Senior High School; Anthony Piscitiello Jr., from Cotter High School; and Mike Brankin, Denise McCabe, Ben Murray, and Heidi Voth, from Saint Mary's University; all located in Winona, Minnesota. After studying hundreds of stories, we selected the forty-six in this book.

Thanks

Great thanks is due to all the students who allowed their stories to be submitted for consideration. The only unpleasant aspect of editing this book was having to omit so many excellent stories. They just could not all go into the book. We thank all of you for your contributions and understanding.

Thanks also goes to the religion and English teachers who sent in the scores of stories received. Your cooperation made the book possible.

The stories contained here are fascinating and moving. They make inspiring personal reading, will serve as excellent discussion or reflection starters, and will find a welcome spot as readings for prayer services. They might even stimulate someone to write their own story. Each story shows how young people display the extraordinary strength and vision required to draw good out of bad situations. We hope that all who read these stories find consolation, inspiration, and great hope.

Neha Lall
Divine Child High School
Dearborn, Michigan

Peace

"Can you feel it?" my mother asked as we stepped out of the hospital doors into the cool night air.

"Feel what?" I replied, even though I had an idea of what she was talking about.

"The peace in the air," she replied. "Your father is at peace tonight."

Yes, I felt peace that night, and a sense of closure to the struggle that had permeated my life for five years. But what had it all meant? When I was ten years old, I had no idea what cancer would mean to me or my family. I didn't even really know what cancer was, although I'm sure I pretended that I understood it all. After all, what are you supposed to do when you are told that your father has cancer and is flying to Houston for special treatments. You are supposed to be strong and mature, and I always was.

But that's not the way the summer after fourth grade was supposed to be. That summer was supposed to be filled with swimming and slumber parties, not hospitals. My parents did a good job of shielding me from the ugliness of the situation. However, they could do little to change the situation we were in, and I was forced to grow up in it. Things got better soon, and by the time school started, we were back at home. Life continued. Our family, our peace, had been restored.

Two years later the cancer was back—this time in the liver. Back to Houston for experimental treatments. I stayed behind

12

this time because I couldn't miss school. And so things continued. My parents traveled back and forth between Detroit and Houston, and I attempted to take on the responsibilities of home.

I remember my mom calling from Houston to ask me what I wanted for my thirteenth birthday. The only thing I really wanted was for my parents to come home. God granted my wish that year. My parents were able to come home a week earlier than expected. By that time I had realized that my family was more important than anything else I could possibly ask for.

But my wishes didn't always come true. The cancer spread—throughout the liver, to the vertebrae, and possibly elsewhere. My parents decided to stop aggressive treatments, and focused on measures to stop the pain—the unbearable, agonizing pain. Soon there was little that could be done. No medicine—not even morphine—could stop the pain. Then, one night, my father lost the feeling in his legs. The tumors along his spine were compressing the spinal cord, and emergency surgery was done. After three months of rehab, he was able to walk with a cane.

In a few months the situation worsened, and he was too weak, in too much pain, or just too frustrated to walk. I knew the end was coming even though no one ever told me that my father would die. They all said he was strong, that he would recover, and that everything would be okay. But I knew better. I was only fourteen years old, but I knew my father was dying. I wasn't scared. I had to be strong for my family. When the end finally did come that night in April, I did feel peace. But I had no idea how much pain was still to come.

Death doesn't come easy to anyone. If my father had died when he was first diagnosed, maybe I wouldn't have felt as much loss. I didn't really know my father as a person then. But through the suffering of those five long years I came to understand him. I realized that daddies aren't as strong as they seem. Even though I was the child, and he was the adult, our roles were often reversed. I took care of him. I understood my father better than most people ever understand anyone. He was far from perfect, but he tried harder than anyone I have ever known.

In those five years I also formed an incredibly strong bond with my mother. She remains the strongest person I have ever met, and I respect her immensely. She is not only my mother, she is my friend, my strength, and my constant supporter. She understands what I have been through, and knows exactly what type of support I need. She realizes the emotional scars will never disappear, but she does her very best to help me heal myself.

My experiences as a child were not always pleasant. I have seen things that no child should ever have to see. I was a little girl who grew up much too fast for her own good. But the suffering has made me the person I am today. I value life and people. I am more sensitive to the needs of others, and I think I am more understanding of other people's suffering. My life experiences have proven that through the dark shadows of life we can grow emotionally and learn to love.

Cissy Paig
Saint Agnes Academy
Memphis, Tennessee

Name Withheld
Saint Raymond Academy
for Girls
Bronx, New York

Desertion

My childhood is a vague period of my life. I don't remember much except for a few events. I lived in a small apartment in the Bronx. I was a blissful, content, and dreamy four-year-old. My heart was filled with great love, and, just like any other child, I was naive, unaware of the heartaches and troubles of the world around me.

I was an only child, the center of my mom's attention. If you looked up the word *spoiled,* my face would be plastered right next to the definition. We had a very close bond that I felt could never be destroyed. I would never have imagined what lie ahead for me. I was to face the two greatest challenges of my life: growing up too fast and watching my mother self-destruct.

When my mother became pregnant, I was ecstatic, anxiously preparing to be a big sister. But once my baby sister made her debut, life changed drastically. I didn't take on the role of big sister; I became a second mom.

My mother couldn't handle the stress and the responsibilities she had. She wanted to escape. I could see it in her eyes. She did escape the only way she knew how—by entering the world of drugs. From that time on, I began to witness things that no child should be exposed to.

The close bond I once had with my mother turned to resentment. My childish spirit became a ghost. The spark in my eyes was extinguished. I was a child who had to grow up before my time, a child who witnessed all the evils and demons drugs create.

One night after my sister and I were tucked in bed, my mother and stepfather stepped out of our house, leaving us alone in the dark. My heart raced, my mind spun, and I was slapped in the face with reality. I got up and sat in front of my television rocking myself, putting up a shield, protecting myself from everything. I didn't want to face the ugliness of what was happening to me.

My mother had always been there to shelter and protect me from everything that bothered me. Now I had to protect myself. I was losing the naive child who lived inside me and becoming a terribly scared five-year-old. I felt abandoned, a feeling no child should experience. After crying myself to sleep, I woke up the next morning, hoping it was all a terrible dream. This wasn't the first or last time it happened. It became a recurring incident. Soon I became immune to the situation. I didn't need anyone. I could take care of myself, I thought.

As the days, months, and years went by, I was introduced to many different unpleasant facts of life. But we dealt with them as best we could. Yet the turmoil came to an end one summer night. It turned our lives around. What seemed to be for the worst really was for the best.

My mom left the apartment once again. She left us alone, as usual, and my stepfather was supposedly at work. My sister and I just sat around watching television, taking care of each other. The hours passed by. We were sweating from the heat. The windows were closed and the phone was off the hook, so no one could get in contact with us. My sister began to cry from hunger. I tried my best to quiet her, but there wasn't much to eat. I found sliced deli ham and began to feed her. My stomach was desperately asking for nourishment, but my sister came first.

I was angry and confused. Why was my mother doing this to us? I dozed off for a while, but was suddenly awakened by a big bang on the door. I fearfully held on to my sister. The bangs continued, getting louder and louder. I felt my heart stop when the door slammed open and these men in blue suits came in. My heart revived when I saw my grandmother behind them. We were rescued.

I walked out the door that night in my grandmother's arms, and I realized how much I loved her. We entered a new sanctuary of love, security, and peace. My sister and I regained our childhood dreams. It was a big adjustment. We tried to erase all that our eyes had seen, but some things just won't go away.

Through the years my grandmother has become the woman I call "Mom," while my mother has become a distant relative who disappeared once we moved.

As a high school senior, I have been able to keep honors in school and to grow from a very shy, isolated child to a very sociable, friendly young woman. I've become a leader, not only at my school, but also in my family. I understood what happened as a child and used it to make me stronger and more independent. It has also made me sentimental, sympathetic, and forgiving. I have forgiven my mother because I know she loved us and still does. I understand that the drugs clouded her judgment.

Now my mother and I are friends, trying to get to know each other. I have two mothers in my life whom I love in different ways, two mothers who have taught me many different lessons of life, two mothers who have shaped me into who I am today. If I had to choose, I would not relive my childhood, but I have taken what was handed to me and used it to my advantage. I lost a piece of my childhood, but gained so much more in return.

Name Withheld
Saint Dominic
Regional High School
Lewistown, Maine

Out of the Darkness

A year ago my whole life changed. I was diagnosed with bipolar disease. This is a hereditary chemical imbalance. Bipolar disease is a cycle of mood swings that fluctuate greatly. The highs and lows go to the greatest extremes. Believe it or not, this is the cause of this story's happy ending.

At the beginning of my freshman year at Oxford Hills High School, I was a normal, happy teenager with a boyfriend from the junior class. We were inseparable and became too dependent on each other.

During the fall, I started playing field hockey and made the varsity team as goalkeeper. I felt on top of the world. That's when everything went wrong. I pushed myself too hard and ended up with a serious leg injury that kept me out of school for about four weeks. I spent the rest of the season on crutches. This is when I had my first real down mood.

I got depressed and wouldn't eat or sleep. I experienced a strange numb feeling that wouldn't go away. My weight dropped tremendously and people started to notice that something might be wrong.

Next, the irritating migraines that I had because of stress started. Week after week my mother and I ventured to Portland in hopes of finding out how to stop these horrible headaches. The neurologist prescribed medication, but nothing helped. There would be days when I had so much energy I thought I could take on the world. Then when I felt depressed I pushed everyone away. No one knew what was wrong when I started to cry all the time.

Winter came, and I felt my worst. I played basketball but never enjoyed it. The competition drove me crazy, and I ended up resenting everyone. The darkness had finally overcome my entire mind and soul. I felt like the walking dead. I was going through the motions, not showing any feelings. I asked my mother to set up an appointment with a therapist. My life was in complete disorder. Lynn, the therapist, tried to help me, but it never worked. I still had the numbness, and everything started to go bad at home. No matter what was said, I couldn't handle it. No one ever guessed that I was severely depressed.

Spring came, and I continued to feel even worse. It was time for softball, and I was actually feeling excitement. The varsity coach was my role model. I wanted to do everything possible to impress her. However, during the tryout period, I did everything possible to hurt myself for a reason I can't explain. Knives, walls—you name it, I did it. There was a power I felt when I hurt myself. I was always being hurt in some way, so now it was my turn.

School was horrible. I had made many enemies. Only my very best friends stood by me. They were concerned, and had every right to be. Every day someone seemed to tell me that I was no good. One day I snapped. There was no way I could handle it anymore.

The health teachers always said that a person plans suicide, but I don't remember planning anything. When my boyfriend ridiculed me in front of a lot of people just for fun, I was heartbroken, and it had to happen on a down day. That afternoon I went home like I always did and went to my room. I sat for an hour or so just looking back on the day. I took a full medicine bottle and stared at it for what seemed like an eternity. Before I realized what was happening, I had taken the whole bottle of the prescription drug. I wrote a short letter to my mom telling her I was sorry and that I loved her. I thought that I was going to die.

I faintly remember my mom running up the stairs saying that the guidance office had called her saying that I was unsafe to be by myself. She saw the empty bottle and screamed. I just kept telling her how sorry I was and how much I loved her. My grandmother called 911, and I was rushed to the hospital to have my stomach pumped.

Even before I was fully awake, I was being taken to Jackson Brook Institute in Portland. I stayed there in recovery for almost four weeks. This amount of time seems short to an average person, but when you're locked in a small unit it seems like forever. This is where the good started to happen. After meeting the other kids, I realized that I had much going for me, and my life wasn't as bad as it seemed. There was no way I would trade lives with anyone in there. The counselors made me feel special.

Currently I attend Saint Dom's, and the transfer has been the best thing for me. The psychiatrist that I see is a great guy. He has taught me all about my illness and keeps me on the right path. Each day is a struggle, but I have to learn to deal with life's ups and downs.

Name Withheld
Villa Joseph Marie
High School
Holland, Pennsylvania

Moms

I can remember that June day as clearly as I remember today. My friends and I had just come back from the corner store and sat down on my friend's steps. My next-door neighbor, Moms, came out when she saw that I had come home. Everyone in the neighborhood knew her. They also knew what she had gone through with her ex-husband, but it seemed like a fact no one wanted to accept.

She was the prettiest lady I ever knew. She had gorgeous blonde hair and bright blue eyes. When we were young, she used to come outside and play tag, baseball, and kick the can with us. And when she took me to the mall or to the zoo, she and I pretended we were mother and daughter. Moms really cared for and loved me, just as she did everyone she knew. But back to that day in June.

Moms asked us if we wanted to walk with her to the playground to walk her dog. I was the only one who could go. As we walked, I sensed a strange bond with Moms. She seemed to have a special glow, and I had never seen her so beautiful. We got home right as the sun was setting. We stood out front and talked a little more until my friends came around. As I was walking away, Moms said, "Beth, be careful, I love you" just as she always had.

I turned, looked at her, and said, "Don't worry, Moms, I'll be safe. I love you too, Moms." These were the last words I would ever say to her.

As we turned the corner at about midnight, we saw the police lights, and for some reason I knew it was Moms that they were there for. Everyone ran to see what had happened, but for some reason my legs just wouldn't move. I stood at the corner for what seemed like years until my friend ran up to me and gave me a hug. "It's Moms, isn't it?" I said. "Just tell me she's okay." But she didn't have to. I knew that Moms was dead.

We walked up the street to the front of her house and there lay a once beautiful woman with gorgeous blonde hair and a body full of energy. She lay very awkwardly, with her head thrown far back. Her body had never seemed so fragile, so thin. She had been bleeding from the mouth. She had been stabbed several times, and the front of her shirt was stained a brilliant red. I couldn't take my eyes off her bloody, mutilated body.

The police came to the conclusion that her ex-husband had entered at about 10:00 p.m. Neighbors had heard a fight, and he killed her sometime after that. When they finally took her body out, I just stood there as if they had also put my body into the van and taken me away. My friends, parents, and some onlookers stayed for a little while and tried to make sense of what had happened.

After everyone had gone in, I stayed and sat on the front curb until the sun came up, not feeling sadness (not saying I wasn't sad), but pure anger. I wanted to hurt someone just as bad as someone had hurt Moms. I wanted someone to feel all the anger and all the pain I felt. Finally I began to weep. For a long, long time I sat there crying.

The wake and the funeral were just three days later. I had gone to the funeral home before everyone else had arrived and asked the director if I could go in and see her. He allowed me to go in, but only for a few minutes because he had to prepare for everyone. I pulled a chair up next to the casket. I looked at her and, even though she looked as if she had put up a struggle, she still appeared as beautiful as she did when I left her that night.

I didn't know what I was supposed to do or say to her. I reached in and just placed my hand on hers. I told her how much I loved her and that no matter what, she would always be a part of my day, just as she had been for sixteen long years. I couldn't get all the words out. Tears welled up in my eyes. I didn't want to cry. I fought against it, but in the end I broke down.

I knew clearly at that moment that a part of me went with Moms. And a part of her forever passed on to me. After the service I stayed with her children in the backyard of their grandparents' house. They were small and quiet in their suits and dresses and their sad, dazed looks.

When I think back, I wonder at how impossible Moms's death seems—someone so energetic and loving taken away in the blink of an eye. The main lesson I've learned from this experience is about death. Death is a central fact of everyone's life, and we all must be prepared. There is a precious balance between life and death. We never realize how many things we take for granted, from something as little as a hello every morning from a stranger, to a lifelong friendship.

Sometimes now I don't like to talk about it. The sense of loss still seems overwhelming at times, but I think Moms passed on her love and caring to the people who needed her and loved her. She had great strength, and the strength was passed to me.

We want people, places, and things all to stay the same, but all growth requires some form of change. Life's changes aren't that bad until we fight them. I tried to fight death, but it wore me down. When we accept the change, that's truly when we grow.

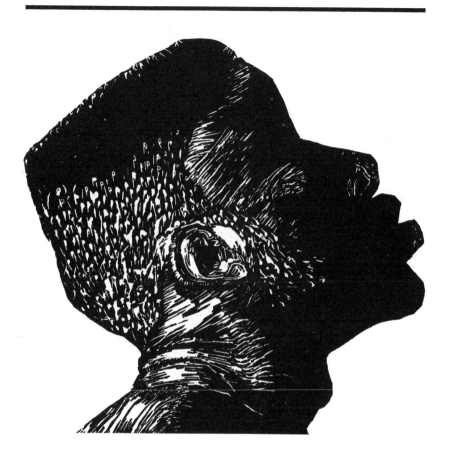

Joanna D'Gerolamo
Saint Agnes Academy
Memphis, Tennessee

Name Withheld
Saint Bernard High School
Fitchburg, Massachusetts

Raking My Way to Knowledge

It is really funny how so many experiences and people in our life teach us valuable things, but it seems like the ones that stick with us are simple, to the point, and come from someone we admire. It also seems that these valuable lessons come out of nowhere. While they are happening we don't think twice about them, but for some strange reason they stick with us. These are the materials from which we grow, though they seem so insignificant at the time. My experience is much like this. It is very simple, to the point, and comes from a man I largely admire, my father.

When I was younger, before girls and my license, I helped my father a little in the yard on the weekends. My father is the type of man who doesn't do anything in a mediocre way. From sweeping to planting, everything has to be done right. He always showed me the way. Back then I did not realize the significance, the big picture. So most weekends I would help my dad, though not always willingly. I never realized the importance and still don't fully, but one time really stuck with me and taught me some important lessons.

I was in the sixth grade. Little League had just begun, and the people who ran the league, all of whose sons played in it, were asking for volunteers to help rake and clean up around the field. I did everything I could to keep this message away from my father because I knew what would happen. Because he was at all the games, of course my father found out. Just as I had predicted, one night at supper my father made it quite clear that both of us were going to go to the field that Saturday morning to help out. I, of course, hated this. I yelled, persuaded, and told him that no kids were going. Still, the date was set and no way out of it.

We went to the field that morning and, just as I thought, absolutely no kids were there. My father and I were assigned a couple of sections to rake. During this time my father did not stop working. Though nothing was in it for him, he worked diligently.

After three hours of raking and complaining, I said to my father, "See, I was the only kid there, that was so bad." Of course I said this in a lousy tone of voice.

My dad looked at me and said two things I will never forget: "If you work and do a good job, people know who to trust. People don't forget things like that." Then he said the second statement that was even more important than the first: "I'm proud of you. You were the only kid. And remember, the more you do, the more you're capable of doing."

These statements were not the only things that taught me. No one worked like my dad that day. Now I see why people always want his help.

A lot of knowledge and lessons came out of this experience and from all the other times I've done something with him, even the things that I detested at the time and probably still would. It's funny, the lessons in my life that I remember aren't from the classroom. They are from doing work as simple as raking with my old man.

Name Withheld
Sacred Heart Catholic School
Morrilton, Arkansas

Second Chance

I am the youngest of nine children, seven girls and two boys. Sometimes we refer to the oldest four children as the first family and the last five as the second. This is because of the age difference between us. Several of the older children were moving out just as us younger ones were beginning to grow up. My oldest sister is twenty-one years older than me and lives in Seattle, Washington. The rest of my family lives in the same town as I do, although I am not as close to some of them as I would like to be.

Anyway, none of us were close to my father throughout our childhood. He was always working, and when he had just a little time off he went to the horse races. My mother raised us basically all by herself, though Daddy supported us. He was always gone to work each morning before the rest of us awoke, and after work he would come home very tired, eat dinner, and go to bed. My brothers, sisters, and I hardly spoke to him. He either wasn't interested or just didn't have time to listen.

My mother served as a link between him and us. When we wanted to do something or go somewhere, we asked Mom. Daddy had nothing to say about it. Most of the time he didn't even know where we were. Oftentimes, it seemed as if we were just burdens on him. He didn't like for us to run around the house or get too loud. We thought of him as being around primarily for disciplinary purposes.

Then my dad had a stroke. Daddy was kept in the hospital for a while, and Mom stayed with him. I'll never forget all of the food people brought us.

After a while Daddy got to come home from the hospital. He was like a completely different person. I remember Mom had to help him walk into the house. My dad was considered disabled, and he was terribly depressed. I saw a side of him that I had never seen before. Many nights when I was lying in bed, I heard him crying to my mother. I just did not know what to think. I had always seen my dad as a strong man. This really scared me.

He couldn't do many of the things that he used to. His eyesight wasn't nearly as good as it was before the stroke, so he couldn't drive anymore. In turn, he quit working. He, as well as my mom, had to drastically change their lifestyles. It was really hard for him, but he did it.

He is fifty-two years old now, and he's home much more. He has grown closer to all of us, especially my mom. They do the daily crossword puzzle from the newspaper together every morning and have gotten really good at it too. They always make a point to watch Scrabble and Wheel of Fortune together, and Mom takes him everywhere he needs to go.

What is really great though is how close he is to my nieces and nephews. They just love him. Sometimes I think that he's trying to make up for not being there for my brothers and sisters by giving their children extra time and attention. I am eighteen now and the only child left at home, so naturally I am around him more than the others. I feel lucky because I have the chance to get to know him a little better than my brothers and sisters did.

I can't help but think that maybe my dad's stroke was a blessing in disguise. I can tell that he really values his relationships with people, and I hope he and I can continue to grow closer every day. I guess it's true what they say, "Better late than never."

Name Withheld
Dominican High School
Whitefish Bay, Wisconsin

Reunion

My brother and I were never very close. It may have something to do with our thirteen-year age gap, but I never quite figured it out. I always knew that I loved him, it wasn't anything like that. We just didn't talk much. I guess you could say we were polite to each other. We acknowledged each other whenever we would see each other. We were just very distant.

My brother moved out when I was about ten, leaving me as the only kid at home. I guess I felt a little resentful about that. Even though we hardly talked, I missed him. He moved in with his girlfriend, and I felt, in a way, replaced. It is so hard to explain, but even though we weren't close, I had a place in his life, and he had an important place in mine. I saw a lot less of my brother after that. I began to forget what he was really like, or maybe I didn't forget. I began to realize that maybe I never really knew him.

Earlier this year something happened that changed both the life of my family and the life of my brother forever. I remember it so clearly that it's almost scary. The phone rang about six o'clock on a Saturday morning. I was, of course, enjoying the extra sleep before I had to go to work. I ignored it. There was no way I was getting up. I let the machine get it. About three minutes later I heard the machine rewind. This meant that the caller must have left a long message. I sprang out of bed and listened to the message.

It was my brother. He didn't sound like himself. His voice was shaky, and he sounded like he was crying. I had never heard my brother cry before. He was begging us to pick up the phone, but I had the volume turned down. He said that the cabin he was staying at up north caught fire. He went on to say that he was badly burned and was being flown to Saint Mary's burn center in Milwaukee.

The flight took two hours, and he arrived in Milwaukee at about eight o'clock in the morning. It was the longest two hours of my life.

We went to see him later that afternoon. I remember having to walk through these huge gray doors into a tiny circular hallway. There were only about six rooms. People were screaming and moaning. Some of the people looked like monsters. The smell was sickening.

My brother's was the first room. When I saw him I almost began to cry. He looked awful. His hair was singed off and his ear was disfigured. His hands and feet were wrapped in big white bandages. He was shaking uncontrollably. He never was big on complaining, so he didn't really say much about the pain. He didn't have to. I could see just how bad it was.

My brother ended up making a full recovery. His strength and will were incredible. I had no idea he was that strong. I spent a lot of time at the hospital with my brother. We actually talked. We got caught up with each other's lives and found out how much we really had in common. It was like meeting a new friend for the first time.

The fire brought my brother and me closer. I can't say I'm happy that the fire occurred, because I'm not. I'm just glad I got to know my brother before it was too late.

Michael Over
Saint Mark's High School
Wilmington, Delaware

Differences

You learn to accept the differences in people more readily when you are different yourself. I've learned this through experience. I have a speech problem that hinders me in oral expression, from reading a book out loud to casual conversation.

Although this problem causes me much pain and embarrassment, I have learned to accept it. I look around me and see the dreadful diseases and handicaps some people have, the poverty that exists, and the depression some suffer, and I know that I am lucky to have a supportive family and friends.

When I was in the fourth and fifth grades I attended a school that holds many bad memories for me. Because of my speech problem, I was called names and became the recipient of many cruel jokes from my classmates. It was hard to get up and go to school each day. I did it only because I had to. I tried not to make fun of the students who were joking about me, even though it would have been easy. What would I have gained by sinking to their level?

Finally, my parents decided I should change schools. They were concerned that I was losing my self-esteem. When I changed schools I met wonderful teachers and made new friends who accepted me without criticism, even though my problem persisted. From my experiences at my new school I learned to appreciate myself. Believing in God made everything easier also. I do believe that God's light was shining on me and helped me get through those early school years.

Although it might seem as though my speech is only a problem in school, it is also a handicap for me everywhere else! Any time I want to say something, whether I'm ordering in a restaurant, shopping, or on the phone, I have to think of words that won't cause a problem. After a while this gets old! Although I've been to four speech therapists, none has been able to "cure" me completely. They just suggest different ways for me to deal with my problem. Some days are better than others.

So far I have presented the dark side of my problem, but there is a positive side. Through my experiences with cruel and hurtful people I have learned to appreciate others in a more understanding way. We are all special in some way. We must learn to accept all types of people. Although I will probably have my speech problem my entire life, I am trying to learn to live with it, and with other people in the process. In all aspects of my life, I try to live by one guideline: "Treat others the way you want to be treated."

Teresa Ann Clancy
Saint Francis Borgia
Regional High School
Washington, Missouri

Venturing into the Woods

During my sophomore year of high school, I prepared the song "I Know Things Now" for auditions of the play *Into the Woods*. The director told me this would be an ambitious musical that mixed classical fairy tales into an exciting adventure in the woods.

As the director gave me an audition tape of the music, my hands trembled, even though it was months before the actual auditions. He seemed surprised that someone would care about putting months of hard work into just an audition. I didn't care though. I listened to the tape, and I discovered which role I wanted—the lead role of Little Red Riding Hood.

I listened to her song "I Know Things Now" over and over again. I made up actions for my audition, thinking that it would increase my chances. Like Little Red Riding Hood, I grew more excited and scared as it came closer to my audition, but I believed I had an excellent chance of landing a role. People who slave over their work and deliver good products usually get rewarded, so I toiled with my audition until it gleamed.

Finally, mid-January arrived along with the *Into the Woods* auditions. I delivered a perfect audition. Nothing went wrong; it was just as I practiced it. Upperclassmen who I didn't know came up to me to say how well I did at the audition and that they were sure I was going to get a leading role. Two days later an announcement was made that the director was holding callbacks. I went to the bulletin board. My name was on the list.

My stomach tied up in knots. I would have to continue practicing the song and actions over the weekend and continue to wait for the final results.

I auditioned again along with about seven other girls. The next day the director posted the cast list. My name was on the cast list as a member of the chorus.

I could have entered the audition completely unprepared and received a chorus part. I swallowed my pride and took the part. After all, as I later found out, "You may know what you need, but to get what you want, better see that you keep what you have."

I tried to forget about my bad experience with the *Into the Woods* audition, but that was easier said than done. Everything reminded me of it. My theater appreciation class spent every day working on the set. The chorus rehearsed once, sometimes twice a week. I had to build sets on Saturdays.

As it came closer to production week, I lived in the theater. I worked on Cinderella's house every day after school since I had to finish it for a grade in my theater appreciation class. Then the student director asked me to finish some essential set pieces that had not even been started. We only had a few days left before opening night, and I didn't think that the set would be finished in time. Finally, after spending hours on agonizing little details, and with only one day to spare, we completed the best set ever built at my high school theater.

If I had received a major role in *Into the Woods*, I may not have met some of my best friends who worked on the set with me. I also wouldn't have worked backstage on more recent plays, and I wouldn't have been student director for the fall play. Most of all, I wouldn't have the memories.

I discovered that I enjoyed being a nervous wreck, fixing broken lights, mixing paint, washing out paint brushes, being stressed on opening night, and appearing on stage even if it was only in the chorus. It gave me an experience that I would not have otherwise acquired without "venturing into the woods."

One high school musical taught me to search for my future, uncover my past, listen to my heart, face my fears, and discover that I am not alone, because disappointment and happiness are both parts of life that each person must go through. One of my favorite quotes from the play sums it up best. As James Lapine and Stephen Sondheim wrote:

> Into the woods you have to grope,
> But that's the way you learn to cope.
> Into the woods to find there's hope,
> Of getting through the journey.

Mandy Rager
Holy Cross High School
Louisville, Kentucky

Name Withheld
Immaculate High School
Danbury, Connecticut

The Turning Around

My aunt was killed by a drunk driver. She was only fifty-five years old, and she left behind five children, one grandchild, and another on the way. My whole family was completely devastated by this senseless killing.

This was the event that changed my father's life forever. From the time that I was born until I was eight years old my father was addicted to alcohol. I was too young to realize what was happening, but things weren't getting any better, so my mom decided to leave him when I was three years old. She taught me that no one could help him unless he wanted the help for himself. He tried three different times to get sober, but he couldn't do it.

A week after my aunt died, my dad was at my grandmother's house. He was drunk. As he was getting ready to go home, my grandmother would not give him his keys. She asked him if he wanted to kill someone like some other drunk driver had killed my aunt. He was stubborn and drove home. By this time he had lost everything—his wife, daughter, business, and all his money. He was living in a single-room apartment above a bar called the Montecarlo.

He arrived at his apartment in a panic-stricken state, believing that he had run over someone and that the cops were following him. He was smashing his fingers in his door thinking that there was someone on the other side. People downstairs heard the commotion and called for an ambulance.

He went through detox for the fourth time, but this time he finally admitted he was an alcoholic. He then went to a halfway house in New Haven and lived there for a year. He was able to get counseling and attend AA meetings daily. They even placed him in a job at the golf course that he would enjoy. He had always been an avid golfer and had worked on the courses as a greenskeeper since he was young. So he was very content with what he was doing.

The boss took a strong liking to him and wanted to see him do more with his life. Through the help of his boss, he enrolled in the University of Massachusetts to get a degree in horticulture. It was a big move from a halfway house into the real world. He continued counseling while still going to school. Then he wrote me a letter explaining everything that had happened and why he wasn't there for me. He said he was very regretful that he had missed all of those years, and that he loved me very much. He asked for my forgiveness. I was too young at the time to understand, so I threw the letter away. I regret that.

It took the death of my aunt to make my father sober up. Today he continues to attend AA meetings, but now as a sponsor, so he can help other alcoholics sober up. He gives speeches and always tells the story of my aunt. His life has turned completely around, and now he has a wife, a two-year-old son, and my forgiveness.

That Which Makes Us Stronger

Tatiana Kazdoba
Villa Walsh Academy
Morristown, New Jersey

When everything seems to be going well, you tend to take for granted the good things in your life: your parents, your friends, your health. You forget the squabbles you've had with your family; you're even nice to your little brother. Then something bad happens, and life drags you into its black hole of depression and sadness. From that moment you're never really the same person you were. Everything around us affects who we are, even if we're oblivious to it. Sometimes it takes a devastating event to make us realize how vulnerable we are. It can make us appreciate how delicate everything is. I, like most, learned this the hard way, through a painful experience that lies close to my heart.

The summer had arrived in its glory—sun shining, heat rising. I saw my family every day, but paid no special attention. After all, they *were* my family. They would always be there, right? In the middle of July, the blur focused into a clear picture. It was another lazy, hazy summer day, so one of my friends, Melissa, equally as bored, invited me to sleep over. I remember everything that happened that night, almost as if it were a movie. We stayed up until four o'clock in the morning, mostly due to high sugar intake. We awoke in time for a lunch of bagels and juice. Calling home there was no answer, so I left a message, presuming my mother was outside.

Half an hour later the phone rang. Melissa handed it to me and mouthed the word *Mom.* I started to say something to the receiver, but her words cut me off. I will never forget her first words to me: "Don't worry. I'm at the hospital. Don't worry, Tatiana, but it's Dad."

At that point my mind froze. I stared at the counter as my mother tried to calm me down. She refused to tell me exactly what had happened, but kept repeating that everything was all right and that she would pick me up in half an hour. Mumbling a "Yes," I hung up the phone.

Numb, I walked into the living room and sat down. Melissa asked me what was wrong, but my mouth refused to answer. Instead, tears found their way to my cheek. Understanding my silence, she walked over and handed me a tissue. She sat on the floor next to the chair and patted my hand, assuring me that everything was all right. Eventually I explained what my mother had said, which drew more of my tears.

My mind was racing from the shock. On the way to the hospital, my brother and mother explained what had happened. Around ten o'clock, my father had been working outside with my brother Greg. All of a sudden he collapsed. My brother yelled to the house, calling for my mother. She rushed out and told Greg to call for an ambulance. My father protested feebly, but collapsed again, this time losing consciousness. Frantic, she held him until the ambulance arrived. Once there, they placed a temporary pacemaker on his chest to regulate his heartbeat. At one point his heart just stopped beating. At the hospital they placed him in the cardiac ward and hooked him up to monitors.

Sitting in the car, the story seemed surreal. The question Why? kept surfacing. My father was by no means feeble. And one poignant thought hit me: He could have died. I could have lost my father that morning, and I would not have been there. A sadness washed over me at that moment, one that never left.

When we walked in he greeted us with a smile—his usual, normal, healthy self. Then the second wave of emotion came. Monitors beeped beside his bed; a wire ran to his neck and disappeared under tape. I bit my lip and fought back the tears as I saw him sitting there surrounded by machinery. He looked small and weak.

The doctors could not pinpoint what was wrong. They couldn't tell us exactly what had happened either, except the obvious. That uncertainty was unnerving. My father stayed in the hospital a number of nights. Finally, after a week in limbo, an answer came back from the lab: Lyme disease.

Once or twice before the summer ended, my brother and I had a talk about what had happened that day. He told me how he had felt, and I was touched by how truthful he was. If I had been there, I don't know what I would have done. He had watched his father fall in front of him. Truthfully, he acted a lot stronger than I would have, and for that, I admire him. We haven't mentioned it since then, but those talks meant a lot to me. It was one of the first times we talked not just as brother and sister, but as friends.

That day not only brought my brother and me together, but the whole family as well. We were more sensitive to each other, and I think we still are. We are more of a family now. More importantly, we've all become friends. We've not only grown to care for each other, but also to respect one another.

As for me, that day brought great change. It forced me to grow and to face a reality I did not want to see. It showed me how much I do love my mother and my father, not only as parents, but as people. For that gift of family and love, I will be eternally grateful.

Allison Hawkins
Notre Dame Academy
Toledo, Ohio

Stephanie Vincens
Cabrini High School
New Orleans, Louisiana

Maw-Maw's Angel

For as long as I can remember, my mom's mother, my Maw-Maw, called me angel. She hardly ever called me Stephanie. I remember when I was little, every time my mom was on the phone with her, I would always say in a sing-song voice, "Hi, Maw-Maw," and she'd answer without fail, "Hi, my angel." I kept saying this even after I was a teenager; I kept saying it until she couldn't answer me back anymore.

During my sophomore year, Maw-Maw was diagnosed with Lou Gehrig's disease, a disease that attacks the muscles and makes them unable to function. She started with neck and shoulder pains, and her voice began to slur because the disease started in her throat. She began writing down everything she wanted to say, and even when she wrote me something, I was still called angel.

As the months went on, her throat could do less and less. She couldn't eat orally anymore, so they put a tube in her stomach to feed her. After a while her legs began to get weaker. First she walked with a walker, then she used a wheelchair, and eventually she was bedridden. She just lay in the hospital bed in her room, getting weaker and weaker. She couldn't do anything; she could barely write to us anymore because everything she wrote looked like chicken scratch.

I knew things were getting bad when she could barely open her eyes. I knew it wouldn't be long before God would take her away from her suffering.

44

On Christmas Eve my senior year, my family and my two uncles' families went to Maw-Maw's, like we did every other year. When it was time to leave, we all crowded around her bed to tell her good-bye. I knew it would be the last good-bye. My grandmother died two days after Christmas.

In spite of the hardship of watching someone I love literally fall apart in front of me for the past two years, good has come out of it. My family has gotten closer than we've ever been, so no one had to deal with this alone. My mother and I became close as well, because we support each other. My grandfather and my uncle have started going back to church. As for me, I now think of my grandmother as my own guardian angel. I talk to her when I just need someone to talk to and I know she hears me. Except this time I get to call her Angel.

Name Withheld
Saint Frances Academy
Baltimore, Maryland

Dirty

Well, it all started a little bit before now on the west side of town. Off and on I was selling drugs, not because there was no money, but my father only gave me what he thought would satisfy me.

So about ten o'clock one night, I called up one of my friends and said, "Like man, this is not cutting it. I need more clothes and more money." I started to get upset. There was a hustler that my buddies and myself knew from a while back. In school his girlfriend gave me his pager number. That next night I was basically doing the same thing and watched some videos.

Later that evening I called his pager, and he called me back. When I picked up the phone, I told him it was me. He said he would pick me up at the Mondawmin Mall.

The next day I saw him, and we greeted each other. He was driving a Mercedes Benz. We got in the car and picked up the boy Little Black from my old neighborhood and another boy named Wayne. The hustler kept the gun while we rode behind them in a hack, and Black had the drugs. We got up to Pimlico Road where the stash house was. We had to make about $1,000, and we weren't even out there all day.

Then I thought about it, "Why am I here? I have two parents that love me and I'm out here doing this." After that I was talking to Black, telling him, but he was just a back stabber because he was in charge of us. He left when the hustler arrived and told him about my idea. Well, when he approached me, he had a gun. But the police came. I was dirty, which means I had drugs on me. I threw them down and walked down this alley. I never came back after that.

The good thing that came out of this whole ordeal is that I know that I don't belong selling drugs, but I do need to get an education in school. This is true, especially here at my school now, because without teachers telling you they believe in you and people telling you when you are in the wrong it could cause a person who is not that strong to be drawn into doing other things. This is one of the very reasons I try so hard in school, because this is the only way I can make it positive.

Brian Lowe
Don Bosco Technical
High School
Boston, Massachusetts

Donations

Two summers ago, I was working for the church near my house. In the back of the church is a poor box where people put money that they would like to donate to less-fortunate people.

By the end of every week, there was usually a substantial amount of money in the box. On one particular Thursday night, the day before the box was to be emptied, somebody broke into the church and robbed the box. The next day the pastor of the church, Father McDounagh, was very upset as he explained that the money was supposed to be picked up by a homeless shelter that afternoon.

I went home that night wondering why someone would break into a church and steal money from the poor. I told my mother what had happened. I asked her why it was that when bad things like that happen, nothing good ever comes out of it.

Days went by as they normally would except that nobody was donating any money to the poor box. As word of what happened got out, people were apprehensive about donating money because they thought that it would just be stolen again. Things got so bad that the following week we did not donate any money because there was not enough money in the box. It looked to me like a bad situation was getting even worse.

After a couple of weeks of meager collections, Father McDounagh was thinking about getting rid of the poor box entirely. He said that it wasn't collecting enough money to

48

donate. Later that afternoon other members of the work staff and I sat down to discuss what we could do to get people to start donating money again. After about an hour with no solution, one of the volunteer workers came up with an idea. He suggested that instead of having people donate money, they could give old clothes or food. Our church had never accepted this before, but Father felt that we could give it a try.

After the first week the donations weren't incredible, but they were enough to donate to shelters. As the weeks went by the number of donations got bigger and bigger.

By the end of the summer we decided to put the poor box back out and still take other donations. People started donating money again and things ended up better than they were before the robbery took place. That was the first time that I saw something favorable come out of something bad.

Megan Keane
Main Catholic High School
San Rafael, California

Closing One Door Opens Another

I was only six when my mother had her first operation for breast cancer. I just couldn't grasp the concept that someone so close to me could be in so much pain and that I couldn't do anything about it. Months turned into years, and we didn't really discuss its consequences.

My mom and I were close, and at times we would only enjoy the day if it was spent together. She could pinpoint my emotions and somehow always gave the needed hug or kiss. To me, she was a woman I wanted to be exactly like when I grew older: smart, funny, caring, giving, and happy. In turn, I made her days bountiful with soccer games, talent shows, and stories.

Before we both knew it, I wasn't a little girl any longer, and I could see Mom's swelling hands, shaking head, and scars from radiation. She was getting sicker, and it seemed the bus was going too fast for anyone to adjust the brakes before it crashed.

I remember our only chat about the topic arose at her last Christmas. I asked if she was going to leave me. Minutes passed and, with tears in her eyes, she told me that she would always be here for me. I smiled and thought that I could never survive without the support she had given me. It was even tougher to think that the year of her death was the year she had pro-claimed, in confidence, that she would feel better. Irony had it that she would die at home, with three of her kids present, a month later.

50

For a long time I hated God for giving someone I needed so much such an evil disease and then taking her away. It took me about a year of sad nights to realize how an experience could take so much away, yet give so much in return. I never knew of a loving bond that could be so strong as the one I share with her right now.

It's strange to think that I'll never have two parents at my graduations, birthdays, and sporting events ever again. But it's also truly amazing to know that I'll always have a power pushing me to excel in school, sports, and my community.

I still talk to my mom and ask her for things like I did before, but now I don't have to worry about her attention not being on me, for she's inside my heart, mind, and soul every day. Sure, everybody wants their mom to hug them, yet to feel strong without her is a feeling of happiness in itself. Sure, the hated disease might have killed her, but what's truly her remains.

Each of us holds a different memory, a different smile, and a different image, but it's the same woman, the one who taught me that living through the dark pushes you to find brilliant light!

Name Withheld
Stella Maris High School
Rockaway Park, New York

Hope in Darkness

One obstacle in my life has been my relationship with my father. Sadly, my father and I constantly bicker and fight. Recently, however, something has happened which has kindled a spark of hope inside of me to put an end to our fighting.

To me, the most important thing in life is family, consisting of my father, mother, three brothers, myself, and my dog. I love each of them beyond a shadow of a doubt. Ironically, I spend a great deal of time fighting with my father. This probably makes me sound like a hypocrite, and maybe I am, but before you judge me, please listen to my side of the story.

Sometimes it seems that no matter what I do or how hard I try, I can't please my father. The majority of our arguments stem from basketball. Isn't it hard to believe that a mere game can mean so much and nearly tear a father and daughter apart? My father treats basketball as a way of life, full of opportunities. On the other hand, I perceive basketball as a game that is good for keeping in shape, having fun, meeting new people, and making friends.

When I play, my father usually comes to watch, and whenever he thinks I have done something wrong, he yells at me during the game. This has been going on since I was in the fourth grade. Needless to say, I am embarrassed when he publicly displays his anger and disappointment like that. However, my father continues his criticism of how I played the game long after the game is finished.

The criticism hurts my feelings and, consequently, I fight with my father. I can take constructive criticism any day, but I feel I can no longer take the destructive criticism that my father doles out. For example, my father makes fun of the way I play sometimes by asking how someone as smart as me can play as dumb as I do.

The game of basketball seems bigger than life to him. When I play badly by his standards, he gives me the silent treatment for a few days, I guess forgetting I'm a human being with feelings. As a result of this everlasting criticism, I get frustrated, discouraged, hurt, and angry.

Because of our continual arguing, our relationship has suffered. For example, we never talk about what I do with my friends, what boys I like, or my opinions on current events. I love my father and wish we had a closer and more understanding relationship than we do right now.

Sometimes I feel guilty when we fight because I owe so much to him. After all, he brought me into this world, puts a roof over my head, food on my plate, clothes on my back, and pays for my education. I don't think he says the things he says to hurt me intentionally, but after a while you would think he'd shut up and stop hurting my feelings. Because he doesn't, I wonder if my father loves me unconditionally. For example, if I were a C student, didn't play sports, and didn't excel in any area, but was still a good person, I wonder if my dad would love me.

Last Christmas Eve my dad told me he loved me for the first time in about four years, and he kissed me on the cheek to wish me Merry Christmas. I don't think I could have received a better present. From there I have obtained a speck of hope that our relationship can get better and maybe we can become close friends. Since then, my dad has agreed not to attend my basketball games until he can control himself. We have begun talking about school, the prom, and other things.

My dilemma is something that I will hopefully surmount. Other people aren't lucky enough to have a living father, a known father, or a father that is still around. Compared to them, I am extremely lucky. Life is short, and my father and I have to learn to put our petty differences behind us.

Natasha Achanzar
Saint Scholastica
High School
Chicago, Illinois

Miss Butterfly

It's hard to describe my sister Nina. She's two years older than I am, and unusually tall for a Filipina. She is a carefree, easygoing, and interesting person. Since birth she has been mentally challenged. My parents didn't discover her abnormality until she was about five years old. I've known her to be this way all my life, but I don't recall how I was told about her condition. She doesn't look any different from anyone else. In fact, no one could ever tell she was that way.

The only problem is that she acts like a child, not in the sense that she sucks her thumb and pouts all day, but in the way that she speaks and learns. She bathes, dresses, and feeds herself. She knows all the basics, but she doesn't have the mental capacity that the rest of us have. She is usually well behaved and can be left unsupervised, but not when it comes to being out in the big world. She needs the direction and guidance that all of us needed once.

Growing up with Nina hasn't exactly been easy. It is an emotional roller coaster for me, my family, and especially for Nina. Many times we lose our patience with her. When she becomes jealous or upset, she does not hesitate to show it in public places. For example, she will cry at the top of her lungs if she wants to go home. She may even throw herself on the ground if she doesn't get her way. Nina will announce out loud her need to go to the bathroom. I hate it when strangers stare.

It's not exactly the most comfortable feeling. I know it's only natural for people to react that way, but I wish they could understand.

These days Nina controls herself and has some understanding of the way she should act in public. We rarely have any problems with her behavior. Still, there are little problems we run into when going out with Nina. Everything goes well until she's asked a question by a stranger: "May I help you?" "What would you like to order?" "That's a nice dress. Where did you get it?" She'll give them a blank stare. If she does answer, she will do so the wrong way or say something that doesn't make sense. I feel embarrassed for her and, selfishly, for myself.

We sometimes make the mistake of scolding her when she does something wrong. We tend to forget that she doesn't think the way that we do. It's hard for us to understand her and for her to understand us. She's not a burden or anything. That's the last thing I would say. It's just that it becomes difficult to cope with her difference.

From this long life-experience, both my family and I have grown. I want to focus more on my personal growth though. As I was growing up with Nina, I went through something most of my friends hadn't. I was always hesitant when it came to introducing Nina to anyone. I was afraid people would laugh at her or think she was strange. As I grew older I became even more self-conscious and always tried to avoid the opportunity to take Nina out with me.

Well, I'm happy to say that along with maturation came realization. Through several retreats, my own thinking, and some very fortunate friendships, I discovered my true identity. One particular time was at a summer service retreat. One of the guest speakers told a story about a young girl he taught who, like Nina, had a learning disability. She had brought joy into his life with her color and her gift of being different. The speaker took out his guitar and sang a touching song about her called "My Little Butterfly." I broke into tears.

I realized how truly blessed I am to have Nina in my life. She is a big part of who I am. Nina adds color to my life. Her difference is a gift.

Ann Marie Hines
Immaculate High School
Danbury, Connecticut

From Isolation to Liberation

At the age of ten, I was diagnosed with pre-leukemia. Before being diagnosed I had to undergo numerous blood tests and very painful bone marrow tests. These tests continued after the diagnosis. I had to miss the last part of my fourth year of grade school and my whole fifth-grade year. The doctors had to search for bone marrow that matched mine, and I was one of the lucky ones! They found out in one round of testing that my younger brother, Daniel, was an almost perfect match.

I was kept in the hospital for weeks before the bone marrow transplant could be done, going through sessions of radiation and chemotherapy. This treatment caused me to lose my hair and to be nauseated most of the time. I was so doped up that I don't even remember receiving my brother's lifesaving bone marrow.

I had to take disgusting medicines for a year after the transplant. I was fed through a tube and kept in an isolation bubble for more than a month. To prevent infections after I was allowed to go home, I had to be isolated in my house for a year, only going out when absolutely necessary. Even then I had to wear a mask and gloves. I was not allowed to eat raw fruits or vegetables, have food cooked outside my house, or drink tap water. But when my year was finally up, all restrictions were off.

I have met many interesting people and made many wonderful friends of various ages, like some of the doctors, nurses, and social workers that helped me through this horrible time. They were caring and never let me lose hope, even in the darkest times of my treatment. They never gave up on me or resented me when I took my frustration out on them. One of my nurses even came to visit and cheer me up during my year of isolation at home. I formed a special bond with these people that helped save me. I still visit them at least twice a year.

Some of the other people that I have had the opportunity to meet are the campers, counselors, and staff at The Hole in the Wall Gang Camp. Funded by Paul Newman's Newman Foundation, the camp is open only to children who have had, or still have, cancer or a blood disorder. The people there are warm, open, and understanding. They are all willing to share their feelings and experiences. And even though the stay at camp is only ten days, I have made there some of the best friends I have ever had. I am able to talk to them about things that no one else would be able to understand.

For young people with cancer the camp is amazing, like a utopia. There are no responsibilities or cliques. Everyone just has fun, it doesn't matter with whom. I can't imagine my life without camp. And when I get too old to be a camper, I am definitely going to be a counselor.

Another good thing that came out of my illness is that I have been able to get more in touch with my emotions. This has led me to write poems and music, and to sketch and draw. I hope that my art will help those that see or hear it to better understand what I went through.

I have greater compassion for those who are suffering, and a much greater respect for those who help them. This respect has made me think about becoming a doctor or nurse so that I can help people that are sick or dying. I want to be there for them, just like people were there for me. Maybe at the same time I would feel like I have started to repay those people who helped me.

I now have a deeper respect for all aspects of life. I take a day at a time, trying to live life to the fullest. I know that everyone has to die and that no one knows exactly when or how. I now realize, also, that God doesn't cause bad things to happen. Some things happen that there are no reasons for, but God will try to help us through them.

Mai Tran
Saint Scholastica High School
Chicago, Illinois

Trying to Look on the Bright Side

In my life I have experienced a lot of good things that came out of bad things. The one I remember most is when I had to leave my country to come to America.

In Vietnam my family lived a very poor life. My parents worked very hard, but we only had just enough food to eat. We never went anywhere, but our family was happy together. At least that was what I thought.

When I found out that my parents had borrowed people's money to buy food, I really hated myself. I had always eaten a lot. I had never thought about my parents. I promised myself that I would eat less every day. One night my dad found me crying outside the porch. He came and talked to me. He said that I didn't have to feel bad about anything because we would go to America one day. Then our family would be happy again.

I asked him how we were going to get there. He said that he had applied to go to America twelve years earlier. Maybe someday the people from the government would call and let us go.

From that day on, I started to have hope that one day an American would be kind enough to sponsor us. America was a country where I could find food and freedom, where people would be happy all the time, and where my family would live in peace, not worrying about anything. Not all hopes and wishes come true.

My country was governed by the Communists. Everything we did, we had to tell the government. Not only that, my dad was a soldier who had fought against the Communists. Every step he took, somebody was always watching him. It was really hard to live under this kind of government. We could have been killed, and nobody would say anything about it. We would be very lucky to get to go to America.

One sunny afternoon our family received a letter. To our surprise, it was from the government. My dad opened the letter. It said that we finally had a sponsor. Ten days later the plane would leave Vietnam to go to America. They sent us this letter so that we could be ready. I was so happy and excited that I couldn't keep the news to myself. I went around and told the good news to everybody in the neighborhood. They were really happy for us. They brought vegetables and fruits to our house to congratulate us and celebrate with us.

Finally the day we had to say good-bye came. All of my friends and neighbors arrived at our house to see us one last time. I really didn't want to leave. I had never thought about leaving my country forever before. I also had never thought about leaving all my relatives and friends behind. They were all that I had. They were the people with whom I had lived all my life. How could I leave them behind? However, what could I do? The only thing to do now was cry and say good-bye.

On the plane to America I tried to look on the bright side. I would meet the sponsors and then tell them how grateful I was. After that I would go home and live happily with my family. We would never be hungry again. I tried to be happy instead of being tearful.

Here I am, in America, a country of which I have always dreamed. I get to live where I want with my family. My sisters and I are going to a very nice school. We get to choose whatever school we want to attend. Then, in that school, we get to choose whatever subjects we want to take. Now I have all the things of which I have ever dreamed. My life is wonderful.

Name Withheld
Delone Catholic High School
McSherrystown, Pennsylvania

My
Serenity Prayer

"Get out of my house, right now! I never want to see you again. You're nothing but a damn alcoholic."

This is exactly what occurred at my house about every two weeks or so. My mother kicked my stepfather out of the house so many times in the past seven years it was ridiculous. The sad part was that he always came back within the next week, and my sisters and I had to act as if nothing ever happened. Experiences like this one could completely traumatize one's life.

First of all, one has to understand that alcoholism is an addiction and a disease, possibly even fatal. No one person can change an alcoholic. Alcoholics have to change themselves. Probably the most difficult thing for alcoholics to do is to admit their alcoholism to themselves.

When my mother first married my stepfather, everything went relatively well. He attempted to treat us with respect, and my sisters and I did the same. Then the situation grew drastically worse. He would return home drunk every night and simply pass out on the couch. He would neither identify with anyone, nor would he do any work around the house. My sisters and I helped out, but there is a limit to how much work young children can do. My mother had to become "Super Mom." She had to be the man and the woman of the house, but one person cannot do it all.

My mother had numerous mental breakdowns. These occurred because she could not handle everything that she was taking on. Face it, having to be both the mother and the father of the house would be exhausting in itself, but along with raising her children, she also had to take care of an alcoholic husband. My mother is a strong woman, but she just could not take it anymore.

The one breakdown, out of many, that stands out most vividly in my mind was when my mom hysterically stormed out of the house one night and did not return for three dreadful hours. My sisters and I were incredibly worried because she always carried nerve pills around with her, and it is extremely easy to overdose. My stepfather had passed out on the couch totally oblivious. My younger sister and I curled up on the chair. I was praying, pleading, "Please let my mom come home soon. I love her very much and I don't want anything to happen to her. Please, please!"

Right now, my mom's nerves are back on track a little better, and my stepfather has been out of the house for about a month. She declared, "It's definite this time. I'm filing for a divorce." I want to believe her, but she has said it so many times before that I do not know if she has enough strength to keep her word. I just try to be there for her and tell her, "Mom, I think you're doing the right thing."

From this bad experience, I began to despise everyone who drank alcohol. It took me a long time to accept that drinking alcohol is all right, as long as it is done in moderation. I also learned that when you love someone you have to love everything about them, not just certain parts. If alcoholics are going to change, they have to change because they want to, not because someone else wants them to.

In conclusion, even though it may sound a little biased, I have a piece of advice to all the people out there: Never marry an alcoholic and don't let your spouse become one. It could be detrimental to you, as well as your children. Take it from someone who lived through it.

Name Withheld
Father Yermo High School
El Paso, Texas

Coping

Where should I start? It still hurts to think about what happened. The wound in my heart is still open, and I think it will never heal.

One peaceful afternoon in the comfortable little house that we shared, my mom and grandmother were resting when my brother and I came home from a hard day at school. As soon as we entered our house, he and I got a big surprise. My very worried mom suddenly started explaining that we did not have electricity or gas, but that this would only last a week or so.

That week seemed very long. Then a month passed without the utilities, and we had also run out of food. We started questioning my mom, but she would not respond. Instead, she left with one of her boyfriends. She had done this before, but this time she did not return. My mom had abandoned us. She left my grandmother, my brother, and me to die.

The three of us trusted my mom. We did not try to do anything about our situation because we believed that my mom would contact us and tell us that the utilities would soon be connected. That went on for another month. We were so naive that we put our lives in her hands again. Even though she no longer lived with us, we kept trusting her.

Another long month passed, and nothing had changed. My grandmother, my brother, and I grew weary of asking our neighbors for food. We were not eating right and all of us lost weight. We all started praying.

62

I asked God to give me the strength and courage to survive without my mom. However, nothing was changing, so I began to lose faith. I wanted to kill myself. The pain was too much for me. I did not know where to turn.

It was then that I thought to myself that God was the one and only person who could help me. I started praying again and things seemed to go much more smoothly. My outlook had changed for the better, that is, until my mom showed up and started lying to us again. Doors seemed to be closing again. I was so close to finding peace, but at the same time, so far.

I thought about how my mom had left us at a most inconvenient time, with a man. I really did not want to hurt her feelings, but I had to. I told her that my school principal had given me the money to turn on the utilities, and that I had applied for food stamps. She became very angry, and to this day none of us have spoken to her.

Some good things have come out of this horrible suffering. My brother and I get along much better than we used to. We no longer fight and have grown very close. The three of us have also become even closer to God than we were before. We trust God with all our heart and soul.

Name Withheld
Mount de Sales Academy
Macon, Georgia

A Breakthrough

When my mother went on a trip to Florida, she made me stay with my aunt. The bad thing for me having to stay with my aunt was that she is gay. I was very homophobic at the time, and I told my mother I would rather she kill me than to make me stay with my gay aunt.

My mother told me that my aunt was the only person I could stay with while she was gone, and that I only had to stay with her for a week. I called up all of my friends to see if I could stay at one of their houses, but none of their mothers would let me stay with them for a week. My mother told me that my aunt was a very fun person to be with and that I would have a pleasant time staying with her.

When my aunt came to pick me up, she greeted me with a hello and asked how I was doing. I told her, "All right." Then I sat in the car without saying anything else. My aunt told my mother that everything would be all right, and we were sure to have an enjoyable time. I laughed out loud, knowing that I was going to have the worst week of my entire life.

On the ride to my aunt's house, I turned the volume of my walkman to the highest setting so I wouldn't have to talk to her. When we arrived at the house, we went inside and ate Brunswick stew and grits that my aunt had made. It was one of the best meals that I had ever had. I told my aunt the meal was excellent, and I was actually amazed that I had enjoyed something at my aunt's house. My aunt told me that she would give the recipe to my mom so that she could make it for me. I thought that was awfully kind of my aunt.

My aunt won my affection when she showed me two 17th-row tickets to the World Series between the Toronto Blue Jays and the Atlanta Braves. I gave her a hug and told her that she was my favorite aunt.

That night I felt terrible thinking that I wouldn't have liked my aunt if she hadn't bought me the World Series tickets. I told my aunt how sorry I was for being rude to her and for not giving her any chance to be a friend of mine because she was a lesbian. My aunt told me she forgave me because she could understand my being upset with her and scared of her because she was different than most people. I told her it would take me some time to feel completely comfortable around her, but I was more comfortable around her than I used to be.

The baseball game was thrilling even though the Braves lost. My aunt and I spent the entire time on our feet cheering on the Braves and conversing. On the way home, I thanked her for taking me to the game and for letting me stay with her for a week. I asked her many questions about her lifestyle and found out it wasn't much different than a heterosexual lifestyle. The rest of the week we watched movies and went out to eat, but every day I became more and more comfortable being around my aunt.

I now talk to my aunt without thinking anything is wrong with her lifestyle, and I realize that fear and hatred of gay people is because of ignorance.

Name Withheld
Saint Mary's High School
Sleepy Eye, Minnesota

Sleepy Eye

When I was about fourteen years old, my parents got a divorce and my oldest brother moved out. My mom worked a lot of nights, so I had a lot of free time and started to get into trouble.

Within the next year I got in trouble with the law about seven times, some misdemeanors and a few felonies. When I turned fifteen, I started to experiment with pot, LSD, and alcohol. A few months later one of my best friends was shot and killed in Saint Paul due to gang violence. This was, and still is, hard for me to accept. After that I got into drugs real heavy and got in more trouble than normal. I think it was because I was so full of anger.

I went to court a few weeks later for something that I had done. They told me that I was going to be sent to the Sheriff's Youth Program, a boys' home in Austin, Minnesota, for a month. When I got there, I hated it. It was like jail, but a little less strict.

During the thirty days that I was there, I swore that I would never get into trouble again. However, three months after I got out I was getting into trouble again. I had another court date, and this time they told me that I was going to be put into a foster home in Sleepy Eye, Minnesota. They did not tell me how long I was going to be there, but it did not matter.

What did matter was that I was not going to be living at home anymore. At first I thought about running away, but then

I decided to give Sleepy Eye a try. This was one of the best decisions of my life so far. By this time I was sixteen and in the second quarter of my sophomore year. I was still into drugs.

I thought that my first day at my new school, Saint Mary's, was going to be terrible. When I got there, the principal was really nice to me; that surprised me. The first kid that I met was also really nice to me. He showed me around the school and introduced me to some of the kids in my grade. The first day was not all that bad; it was kind of fun.

That summer the football coach hired me to work for him at his plumbing shop. I played football that fall. I started to become really good friends with a lot of people at this new school, and I started to like it. But I still felt out of place, like I did not belong.

So I decided to go through a treatment program for my drug use to see if I could quit. This was really hard because I told my foster parents all the stuff that I had done that they didn't know about. About two months later I finished the program and have been straight ever since.

After that I felt like I was more a part of the school. I fit in better. The next summer I worked for the football coach again and also played football. Unfortunately, I tore a ligament in my knee, ending my football and basketball seasons for my senior year.

Although I have been involved in a lot of bad things, I know that God has been watching me and taking care of me. I got the chance to leave the bad environment that I was in and make more of myself than I ever would have done in my hometown. That bad day in court enabled me to meet a lot of really neat people. I got first runner-up for homecoming king and a leadership award for football. I'm getting my education. My relationship with my mom and dad is better than it has ever been. I quit my drug habit. And I have a great girlfriend who respects me for who I am now and not for what I used to be. So, for me, good things came out of bad things, thanks to God.

Matt Kruger
O'Hara High School
Kansas City, Missouri

Lessons About Real Life

On a Saturday in December, I woke up at about 6:00 a.m. to get ready to leave for a wrestling tournament in Harrisonville, Missouri. I was aching. I had a slightly sprained wrist and ankle, and my knee had been bothering me for weeks. I hadn't gotten much sleep that night due to my brother's sleepover birthday party, and I was moving pretty slowly toward a long day. Lesson number one: Sometimes when the going is hard, you have to try as hard as you can to keep moving.

I got to O'Hara, my high school, at about 7:00 a.m., met my teammates, and we left for Harrisonville. When we arrived, the first thing we saw was a woman wrestler who was competing in the 103-pound weight bracket. A lot of people were pretty shocked to see her, and many coaches were speaking of forfeiting any matches against her. However, she did wrestle all five of her matches and, even though she lost, showed some definite talent. Lesson number two: Even when the social standards are against you, going out and doing your best shows real character and courage.

I wrestled five matches and went 4-1. This was good enough for me to tie for first place. The coach told me before the tournament that I could do it, and I believed that I could. Lesson number three: A little belief in yourself can go a long way. Hard work pays off.

Shortly after I won my first match, I was approached by a wrestler from one of the competing high schools. His name was Nick. We talked about the tournament and ourselves as wrestlers and how we thought we were doing so far. When we discussed our weight class brackets, we realized that we had to wrestle each other in the third round. I didn't let it bother me, and we continued to talk throughout the day. When it came time for us to wrestle, it felt a little odd because I was expected to beat my friend. He was the only guy that beat me. After it was over, we were able to smile and shake hands with no hard feelings. This was a pattern with the other people I wrestled throughout the day as well. I could talk to them afterward without any hard feelings. Nick is the guy I tied with for first. I couldn't have tied with a better guy. Lesson number four: Good sportsmanship brings more enjoyment to sports, and a good attitude toward people can make even a loss less painful.

I arrived back at O'Hara with my first place medal at about 5:00 p.m. My dad came and picked me up. On the ride home, he told me that my great-grandmother had died, and that my grandmother fell down some icy steps and was in the hospital. He said that my mother was going out of town for the week to be with her family, and that I would have to help a lot with watching my brothers. I was having such a wonderful day up until that point. He said that my mom was pretty upset, but when she heard about my success, her spirits lifted a bit. Lesson number five: Sometimes things happen that are out of our control. We should try to deal with them as well as our emotions can allow.

When I got home I was feeling kind of low and was thinking about a friend of mine that I had been in a fight with over the past week. I called her and apologized for the things I had said and so did she. She was as eager to make up as I was. Lesson number six: Your true friends will always understand the less-intelligent things that you may do.

After that I ate dinner and went to a dance at school that I hadn't planned on attending. I thought that it was going to be boring. I actually had an okay time. It helped me cheer up to see a bunch of friends and get some recognition for my tournament performance. Lesson seven: You can always take comfort in friends. A pessimistic attitude is likely to be false when dealing with the people who care about you.

After I got home, I worked out for about twenty minutes. I had eaten some pretty bad things, and I needed the workout. I was tired, but a workout before I go to bed usually helps me sleep. Lesson eight: Always try to better yourself, even when it seems that you can't go any more.

Shawn M. Beirne
Holy Cross High School
Louisville, Kentucky

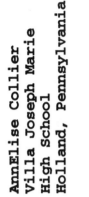

AnnElise Collier
Villa Joseph Marie
High School
Holland, Pennsylvania

The Night

An average American family living in Allentown, Pennsylvania: a father, a mother, and two young girls. They were just starting off and had saved enough money to buy their first house. The father had finished medical school and was completing his internship at a hospital. He and two of his medical associates had decided they were going to open a family medical practice center. It was going to open in a few weeks.

Jerry and Lisa went out late one night and left Mary Grace, three, and AnnElise, one, with a babysitter. Just when they returned, Jerry got an emergency call from the hospital. He decided to take the babysitter home and answer the call. Lisa went to check on the children, and when she saw that they were sleeping soundly, she went to bed.

Early the next morning, Lisa was awakened by a police officer banging on the door. He was the bearer of only bad news. Jerry and the babysitter had been hit by a teenage drunk driver. The babysitter sustained serious injuries, but Jerry was killed instantly.

This tragic story isn't about me, AnnElise, or Mary Grace. It's really about our amazing mother. A young widow, only in her twenties, had to deal with a tremendous loss and face the challenging task of single parenthood. She had no job and no college degree. In her teenage years, she had turned down two college scholarships. In marriage she and my father became totally dependent on his salary. After his death she had to learn to be independent. With two kids and no income, she really had no choice.

For about a year her parents, who lived in Philadelphia, came up almost every day and stayed at the house on weekends. We qualified for social security, and for a while we lived on those checks and financial help from the family. My mom decided she needed to move away from the bad memories, so we moved to northeast Philadelphia. We lived in a one-floor twin house with two bedrooms.

My mom borrowed from the bank so she could go back to school. She attended Holy Family College and got her degree in elementary education. Between gymnastics, music lessons, and bank loans we were barely making ends meet, but she would never let us know that. She got her first job as a Catholic school teacher, and we lived on her meager salary for a while.

After the accident, three lawsuits slowly made their way through the courts. It took nine long years for the courts to settle them. Unfortunately, this meant nine years of waiting and testifying for everyone involved, including my mother. Not everything came out in our favor, but with the conclusion of the legal aspects, my mother now had time to deal with the mental and emotional aspects.

She found satisfaction in teaching, but she knew she didn't want to teach all her life. She had met some friends who were also young widows and widowers. They formed a small support group, but it wasn't very long-term. Then we moved to Holland, Pennsylvania. She quit her teaching job and took a part-time position as a secretary, so that she could go back to school. Money was tight, but we managed. Reflecting back on that small support group, she decided to get her master's degree in counseling psychology. While doing her internship, she met John T. Jastremzski. She had not dated in over eight years, but she wasn't afraid anymore. She and John got married that same year, and he is a wonderful addition to our family.

After her graduation, she and another graduate friend opened a business, The Counseling Network for Loss and Transition. They specialize in counseling young widows and widowers. She now helps people to deal with what she dealt with. To be that strong, to be that supportive, to be that independent, to be that brave, and to still have all the time and love in the world for her two daughters is, to me, simply amazing.

Name Withheld
Saint Catherine Indian School
Santa Fe, New Mexico

My Storybook

As we grow up, we learn life is not what it seems to be in the storybooks. We have opened a new storybook, reality, full of personal stories, some of which may be harder to talk about than others. In this book there are still blank pages waiting to be filled by events in one's life. The stories are full of love and peace, war and violence, racism and injustice, happy times and sad times, dreams, wishes, and goals.

I grew up in a family of six. Being the youngest was diffi-cult at times. On my dad's side, the families got along well enough to keep everyone happy, but we did not have a bond like some families do. We all lived near one another, but I yearned for that bond of closeness.

I grew up and started school. I learned a lot, not only about school subjects, but also about how the world is. One person in our family, older than most of us grandchildren, was maturing and entering a new world of her own.

One night I was at my grandma's house. I loved to spend time there, and especially to talk to this person who lived there. She and I were almost like best friends back then. The time that evening passed quickly, and all too soon I realized that it was late. I decided that I should be going home. She asked me to stay with her because she was bored and had nothing to do. I thought about it, but decided that it was time to go home. So I left.

I wish that I had stayed. As I slept that night, other things were happening. After a while I heard voices in our living room. I got up and went to see what was going on. I remember my mom running out the door. I followed after her.

We entered my grandma's house, and there was my friend lying on the couch, unconscious, cold, and pale. She had been raped. The ambulance was called. The police came looking for evidence.

It seems that after I left, my friend either got a phone call or she called someone, and then decided to go out. My grandma said that she heard a knock on the door and a car drive away. Later she found my friend lying on the back porch.

I felt so bad afterward. All I could think was, "Why her? I should have stayed. If I had, this would not have happened. It's all my fault."

Two weeks later she was brought home from the hospital. No one was charged with rape. When I looked at her I knew that she knew who had done it. As the days went on I tried to make her happy. I was so thankful that we had found her.

Now she is doing great. She is very much her old self again, but she protects herself more. This incident has made me grow up and realize that anyone can hurt you. I now watch after myself more and make sure I don't give anyone the wrong idea. I am happy with the relationship I'm in with my boyfriend because I feel safe with him. He treats me well and takes care of me. I trust him and he trusts me.

I have also come to realize that some families do grow much closer and come to have strong bonds in times of need.

Name Withheld
Saint Scholastica High School
Chicago, Illinois

Illuminate

My parents were divorced when I was seven. I was molested when I was eight. My parents both remarried very quickly— eight months after their divorce. I was diagnosed with an ulcer when I started my freshman year of high school, and I was date raped when I was sixteen. These experiences were never discussed, in my head or with the people around me. I spent sixteen years feeling like there wasn't a single thing in my life that I could control. Then I found something to control.

I started bingeing. I would eat mass quantities of food and then realize I couldn't bring myself to vomit. So I turned to blatant starvation. I was controlling something. I said what went into my body and when. I was often faint or dizzy, but I was in control. The pain in my stomach was something I could understand, something to relate to. Watching the numbers get lower and lower as I stepped on the scale was a rush. I got off on malnutrition.

People around me noticed my obsession, but, much to my pleasure, they couldn't do a thing about it. I thought that I had finally figured out a way to live for me and not for everyone around me. I was paying attention to myself. I had taken my life into my own hands. But what I hadn't realized was that I not only had my life in my hands, I was hanging on to it by a slender thread.

Sometimes I would lay on my back and make sure I could count my ribs. Why I thought that I was becoming happy, I don't know. I can remember a time when I cried hysterically until I lost my voice and coughed blood. I think anorexia is like alcoholism. It doesn't really make you feel any better, but it gives you something to concentrate on other than the pain in your heart.

For a long time everything around me was pretty bleak. For a long time I didn't let myself see the darkness. I think this caused a little part of me to go insane. I had to let my world in my head get really black before I could see clearly. I let myself mourn by showing people what pain looked like. Five feet eleven inches, 110 pounds—that's pain. That's sixteen years of pain shed away with forty-two pounds of flesh.

It's taken a lot of talking and time, but I'm coming to grips with my past and dealing with my present. I know now that my problem isn't weight, it's my way of life. Feelings I can deny, appearance is unavoidable. I don't regret what I did to myself. Some people cry when something goes wrong, others put their fist through a wall. Me? I've always shoved it inside, given everyone around me a shoulder to cry on, picked them up, and moved on. I wasn't letting myself be human. It was inevitable that I would fall apart. I guess I was making up for lost time. The memories are painful, but I had to let myself see the darkness. From that I've learned to truly appreciate the light.

Dairrick Jordan
Archbishop Carroll
High School
Washington, D.C.

Thanksgiving

During my volunteer work for the Thanksgiving food drive, I journeyed from house to house asking for donations of food, expecting the worst, of course.

First I went to my next-door neighbor who I'd never had a formal conversation with until that day. I ran into the man of the house. After my explanation of my request, he looked at me as if I were asking him for his life. He seemed frightened, hurried, even anxious to get inside and away from me. This struck me as peculiar and insulting. Then I began to think about it. I put myself in his shoes; I tried to rationalize why he would be afraid. Was it me or was it the idea of giving up something? a few cans of food? a box or two of dried goods? Even after twirling the idea around inside of my head, investigating his motives, thinking of what could possibly provoke such a reaction, trying my best to interpret his actions as something better than outright selfishness, I still could not come to a justifiable conclusion. So I gave him the bag and the flyer and left, totally discouraged, thinking that my first encounter would set the tone for the rest of the evening.

I continued my journey in hopes that I would be able to collect a suitable amount of food for the drive. After an hour or so of leaving bags at many houses, I moved on to another street where I was blessed enough to find a church that was overjoyed to give. They gave me a whole stack of food. I wish that I could have done more or said something more than "Thank you," but I didn't. Why? Now that I think about it, I think they could see the adoration in my face. They could see how happy I was to receive their donation. Now, every night, I say a prayer for that church, asking God to bless them and to fulfill their needs, just as they fulfilled mine. It's all that I can think of to repay them for their generosity.

The last house I visited was new to me. I'd never been there before. As a matter of fact, before this encounter, I thought it was abandoned. When I went to knock on the door, I didn't know what to expect. Suddenly a woman answered the door. She was a nice lady in her late twenties, blonde, very attractive. When I began my recitation of the "Thanksgiving Donation Creed," she began to look at me in a very peculiar manner, almost as though she were staring at me. I thought that she was going to treat me just as the gentleman I encountered earlier had treated me, but she didn't.

She was partially blind. When I finished with my routine, I almost felt embarrassed asking her to give up anything, but without any hesitation she answered me with an enthusiastic, "Yes! I would be delighted to help." At first this amazed me. I wanted to ask her why she would be so willing to give away anything when it seemed like she was already missing so much, but I didn't. I accepted her offer and left the bag with her. The next day, when I went to collect the bags, hers was the first I wanted to check. When I got there I found two bags, each filled to capacity with everything for Thanksgiving, from cranberry sauce to stuffing.

This experience showed me that in a world full of darkness there is always hope. I encountered so much ill will and selfishness from those that had more than enough, and so much generosity and contentment from one who seemed as though she would never want to share what she had with the world. This one person's actions sparked a flame of hope inside of me. I can only hope that there are more people like her in the world.

Elizabeth Pereira
Academy of Our Lady of Guam
Agana, Guam

After the Accident

I opened my eyes and found that one of them had been covered with a patch. I looked around and soon realized that I was not at home, but in a hospital room surrounded by family members. Although I could not see my dad, I could hear his voice. I called out to him and tried to sit up. My godmother comforted me and kept me from moving around too much because of IV tubes. My dad assured me that everything was going to be just fine. I was too weak to argue, so I believed him and went back to sleep.

The next day I was moved to my brother's room. That was the first time I had seen him since the accident. He was wearing a cast because he had broken his wrist. I asked questions about my mom and tried to find out why she wasn't there. No one wanted to tell me anything except that she was okay and that we would soon be able to see her. The following week we were released. My dad was staying in the hospital with my mom, so my brother and I had to stay with my godmother.

The next few months were an adjustment period for me. Going back to school was really hard. My classmates constantly asked questions like, "Where did you go?" and, "What happened?" A few of them teased me about the bandage on my eye; they called me "One-eyed Lizzie." I didn't know how to respond to their questions because I barely remembered the incident myself, and I was too weak to respond to their cruelty by fighting back. So I tuned it out as best I could.

Several months passed before all my mother's operations were completed. Our family moved in with my mom's mother because our apartment was not prepared for a person in a wheelchair. My brother and I had to learn to work with my mom's disabilities. Several changes were made around our house to accommodate her. My brother and I took on twice as many chores as before. I had to learn how to cook, clean, and wash clothes. Since most of my time was spent caring for my mom and my brother or keeping up with my chores, I barely had enough time for anything else.

My dad worked long hours, and my grandmother owned a floral and bridal shop, so no one was available to take me and my brother to places we wanted to go. We were not able to go out with our friends, join any clubs or teams, or participate in extracurricular activities. The limits on time and support were not the only reasons why we were not able to take part in any of these functions; the lack of funds was another contributing factor.

My dad was the only person in our household who was working to support us. Our hospital bills were overwhelming. Sometimes our meals were just enough to feed the four of us. To make it worse, my brother and I were both attending a parochial school that required monthly payment for tuition.

This whole ordeal taught me a lesson or two, and helped to make me the person I am today. When the accident happened, I was seven years old and my brother was five. I learned to cook and clean while most of the other second graders were dependent on their parents for these services. Because of my situation, I was given an opportunity to learn to depend on and support myself. Because my mom was in a wheelchair, I learned how to work with a disabled person. Most of the children at my school had pretty clothes and nice toys; I learned to make do, to go without. Everything I was forced to learn in order to adapt to my bad situation has helped me deal with many other difficult circumstances; all my acquired skills are still useful to me now. As I look back on those few years of hardship, I realize how much I had grown in that short time.

Christina Fandal
Cabrini High School
New Orleans, Louisiana

My Special Friend

I met my special friend, whom I will call Annie, when I was fourteen. She was sixteen at the time and dating my older brother. I only knew her as his girlfriend. However, the following summer my mother took me, my brother, Annie, and my cousin to Florida. We took walks, and we would sit on the beach at night and talk for hours. We developed a mutual respect for each other and our friendship began.

Shortly after our trip, Annie and my brother ended their relationship and, because it was an awkward situation, we did not see her for some time. One evening Annie came by to tell us how much she missed being a part of our family. My mother told her that we did not have to end our friendship because she and my brother broke up. My mother told Annie that she was welcome in our home.

Annie and I began doing things together. We always had fun. She had a stressful home life. Her mother had been married several times and had two young babies. Annie went to school for half the day and worked until the evening. When she came home, she would take care of the babies. Even when my brother was dating her, she could not go out on weekends because she had to baby-sit while her mother went out. At times she would spend her money buying food for the children.

I loved going to her house to help her with the babies. I became very fond of the children and sometimes would baby-sit for her so she could go out on a date. My friend never complained. Annie's only concern was for the well-being of her two siblings.

The happiest time should have been Annie's senior year in high school. However, her stepfather left her mother, and one day when she came home from school her mother told her that she was leaving to go back to live in her hometown in another state. She told Annie to find a place to live. They argued.

Annie called me crying, "What am I going to do, where am I going to live?" Her mother told her that no one loved her and no one would be at her graduation. Two days later, when Annie returned home from working, the house was empty. Her mother was gone. Annie was frantic.

I called my mother at work, explained what had happened, and asked my mom if we could keep her. My mom replied, "Honey, she is a human being, not a pet."

When Mom came home, she talked to my father. Dad said, "We always have so many children in this house, we probably would not even notice if we had one more." My parents had never met Annie's mother and knew very little about her. All they knew was that they could not leave Annie in the street.

My mother found the address of Annie's biological father and wrote to him. A few weeks went by before my mother received a letter from Annie's father and grandmother. They thanked her for showing so much love and generosity to someone who was almost a stranger. Annie's grandmother called my mother and told her that for years her son had wanted to have a relationship with his daughter. However, he had many medical problems and, because Annie moved around quite often with her mother, it was difficult for him to keep in touch.

Instead of graduation being an unhappy event, it was very special. Annie's mother did not come, but her father and grandparents did! I will never forget the look on her face. Her eyes glowed, and she was smiling from ear to ear when she walked down the aisle and glanced toward her father, grandparents, and the rest of us who were there for her. If her mother had not left, the rest of her family would not have been there.

The class turned around, faced the audience, and sang a beautiful song. My mom took a picture of Annie as she gazed toward her father and his parents. After the graduation we went out to eat, and my friend held her father's arm the entire time.

Annie's grandparents and father spent a week with her and asked my mother to try to persuade Annie to live with them. I did not want to let her go because I had finally gotten the sister I had always wanted. However, my mother said that Annie had never had the opportunity to be carefree because she had always had so much responsibility. We also had to be realistic. She needed a car, a job, and college. Her grandparents would help her as much as possible financially if she decided to give them a chance.

Annie went to live with her grandparents and father. She survived the pain. Annie's experience taught her to be independent. She did not resort to alcohol or drugs. Instead, she showed me what courage was all about. She has visited me once, and we correspond by letters and phone calls. She has a full-time job and her own apartment, and she is attending college part-time.

Bad things happen to all of us in life. But it is not the bad things that cripple us, it is what we do about them. I was affected in a positive way by Annie. I realized what a safe, secure haven my home is. I had taken my parents for granted because they had always been there for me. Most of all, I realized that true charity comes from what we give of ourselves to help other human beings, and true love is giving a person the necessary tools (love, support, education, and encouragement) and letting them go, so they too can survive and fly alone.

Amy Brookshire
Saint Agnes Academy
Memphis, Tennessee

Anthony Vitanzo
Saint Peter's Prep
Jersey City, New Jersey

Cheerful

The person I most admire in this world is my brother Philip, who is thirteen years old. He has many attributes, but the one characteristic I most admire is his courage.

He has had to deal with numerous physical problems. When Philip was born, my mother and father did not know if he would live or die. He was five weeks premature, only five pounds at birth, and he had many strikes against him. But even though he was that tiny, he proved he was a fighter. Through Philip's perseverance and determination, he was able to come home with my parents and me.

Life with Philip wasn't easy. He constantly needed medical attention, and many times he had to be hospitalized for different ailments and infections that were life threatening. Finally at age seven, Philip had the first of many surgeries. Philip actually needed three surgeries simultaneously. His surgery lasted eleven hours. Afterward, my parents took turns staying by his bedside. At one point Philip received the anointing of the sick. My father was only off of work on Sundays. On Saturday night he would relieve my mother so she could come home, wash up, and spend time with me. This went on for weeks.

Philip always seemed to be in discomfort. It wasn't easy for my parents to watch this, and it was very hard for my father to concentrate on his work. My mother was so consumed with getting Philip better that she felt she sometimes forgot about me.

86

But my father and I would visit Philip almost every day and try to cheer him up, or we would just spend time with my mom. The surgeries continued over the years, and his courage became more evident. On many occasions I would have given up, but not Philip. He always seemed to pull himself on top. He has this ability to make a very bad situation into something positive.

Seeing Philip face life every day gave me the strength I needed to concentrate on my schoolwork and to try to make my life as normal as possible, even though I knew my parents were preoccupied with my brother. I thank God for the many family members and friends who helped us through those rough times, and who gave me the attention I needed so my mother and father could be with Philip.

Today my brother Philip still has some problems, but because of his courage he is able to face each day as it comes, conquer any fears he might have, and meet each surgery with a renewed sense of hope. His courage has made him a stronger person.

I'm grateful to my brother Philip for teaching me the meaning of courage, and I am thankful to God for giving me the privilege of being his older brother.

Name Withheld
Reicher High School
Waco, Texas

Rock Bottom

During my life, I have had the good fortune not to encounter many major mishaps, but there have been some painful ones. When I was young, I suffered from a small amount of child abuse. Although I didn't have very many bruises to show, my emotions were black-and-blue. As I grew older the physical abuse lessened, but the emotional abuse increased. I am a tough person, and I am also a very good actor, so good that I fooled myself for many years. I forced myself to believe that this was a way of life, and that I should just live with it.

As I grew, my hurt and anger grew deep and great inside me. I was always holding my feelings and thoughts inside my mind and heart. One day I couldn't deal with the world, life, or anything anymore. I tried to kill myself.

At the time, that was the only way out that I could think of. I had tried to do this to myself many times, but I had never had the courage to be very aggressive. I was crushed with emotional hatred for the world, along with everybody in it. I was angry at God, and many times I found myself asking God what the purpose was of my being here on earth. I thought no one cared for me or loved me. When I tried to do what I did, I thought that I would be doing myself and the rest of the world a favor.

I was lucky enough to be near a caring and loving adult when the event took place, and I was immediately taken care of. After putting up an enormous fight, I was rushed to the nearest hospital. During my trip, I slowly and subconsciously realized that what I had done was wrong, and that I was just frightened and confused. I didn't know how to handle or juggle my emotions and feelings anymore. I was trying to take the easy way out. Believe me, it never would have worked.

When I reached the hospital, I went through a long series of examinations that made me regret all the more what I had tried to do. I felt like a little kid, lost and scared in a strange place, and I wanted my mother to hold me and comfort me. That was not possible. I was many states away. I have often heard the saying, You got yourself into this mess and now you've got to get yourself out. I thought that I would have to face my fears all alone.

I was wrong. Many people that I knew and people I didn't know were there to help me through it. One of the nurses said to me, "I know you didn't know what you were doing, and that you didn't really want to end your life. You were just trying to find a way to scream to the world 'help'." I had never thought about that before. Right when I heard it, I knew that what she said was true. It shocked me. All this time I really was looking for a way to ask for help.

People say that when you reach rock bottom there's only one way to go, and that's up. They are right. From that point on, I began a new life. I have learned to express my feelings and thoughts. I am now a better person, and I am grateful that God gave me this burden, for out of it came my ray of sunshine, my hope.

Dennis Wilson
Billings Central Catholic
High School
Billings, Montana

Don't Judge

I had just turned fifteen. My family and I were coming back from visiting my grandparents in New Mexico. We were driving my aunt back to Missouri. I considered myself to be fairly intelligent and aware of the world and the people in it. But I didn't know how stereotypical my thinking was until an incident changed me.

We were driving through Kansas City when we needed gas and had to stop. We took a wrong exit and found ourselves driving through what seemed to be an all African American area. We pulled up to a stoplight, and our car broke down! I don't remember quite what I said, but it must have been something like "Let's get out of here!" because I remember the fear that I felt.

My dad got out, popped the hood, and tried to figure out what was wrong. To make it even more uncomfortable, we seemed to be the only "light" people around. My father is an American Indian, but his complexion is quite light. I could hear racial slurs being yelled at my "white" father. I couldn't imagine any way out of this mess.

Just as things seemed really desperate, a car pulled up and an older black man and woman got out, helped us figure out what was wrong with our car, and got it started. Then they followed us out of town and made sure that we were all right.

I'll always remember that incident. I felt totally threatened, but I stopped thinking in stereotypes. Even when I do start thinking in the old patterns, something happens or some person comes along and changes it all again.

Amy Westerman
Holy Cross High School
Louisville, Kentucky

Shannon Anderson
Mercyhurst Preparatory School
Erie, Pennsylvania

"All Things Work Together for Good"

Even though it is sometimes hard to see the good in a bad occurrence, it can be evident in certain ways thereafter. For me, one such event would be when one of my friends was killed. I am still struggling to understand why things like this happen, but I do know that some good has come of it.

About 9:30 one June night, I was talking on the phone to my friend Tabitha. I heard a sound outside that I thought was dead wood being run over by a passing car. The sound was a little suspicious, so I got up, looked out the window, and saw a car pulled over at the side of the road. My mother went outside to see what had happened. I was not really scared until I heard someone scream.

Across the road, my mother picked up the phone in the milk house of our family's farm. She told me that it was an emergency and to hang up, which Tabitha and I did immediately. My Aunt Barb brought her two children, ages five and three, for me to take care of while she went out to help.

At first I thought it might have been an animal, like one of our cows or a dog. Then when I looked out the window into the night, I saw the figure of a person lying on the ground. I heard someone shout, "She's been hit!" and I got really scared. I still did not know who was hurt and what had really happened, but the next thing I remember was seeing the ambulance stop in front of our house.

92

My mother came back in the house to get a flashlight, and she told me that my neighbor and friend, Kathleen, had been hit and was injured very badly. My two little cousins kept asking me what had happened and who was hurt. I wished that they didn't have to know, but I told them that Kathleen had been hit by a car. They were both very shocked that it was someone they knew well, even though they were only five and three years old.

After a long time of waiting and watching the police fill out reports, the ambulance left, and the lady who hit Kathleen was driven home because she was completely devastated. I could not sleep that night, and the next day I was unemotional. Why did this happen? I'm still trying to figure it out.

Kathleen was only twenty years old. She had a lot of talent, but never found the right place to use it. She was still searching her soul for answers, but never got a chance to find them. Was there any good that came out of this horrible incident? Why did it have to happen? The answers to these questions may never be known, but I do know that this tragedy has caused me to think a lot about life and what it means. Kathleen's death has taught me to use my time on earth wisely, to value my life, and to do good things while I have it. It has also shown me that life can end at any moment. I am more aware now that I need to improve my life and the way I live it in order to get finished with what I am placed here for.

I still find myself wondering why someone had to die to show others the importance of life. The best answer I can find is from Romans 8:28, "We know that all things work together for good for those who love God, who are called according to his purpose." For now I will enjoy the present and look forward to the future and to what I am called to do.

Name Withheld
LaSalle High School
Pasadena, California

Why?

About seven years ago, a major change occurred in my life. Yet to this day, I still do not know if it was for the best. When I was nine years old, my parents got divorced. I loved both of them, but I also hated them because they were doing this to me. My mother moved out. I then lived with my dad whom I had hardly ever talked to before the divorce.

At the end of the school year, my father and I moved to another city. Life was very hard for me. I had only one parent, and I had lost the other one that I cared for so deeply. And to make things even worse, we moved to a new city where I literally had no friends. My life seemed horrible. I can remember asking God why this was happening to me.

My father remarried. This made me extremely unhappy. First, I did not like the woman he was marrying and, second, I felt that she was trying to take my mother's place. I cried and yelled at my father for doing this, and again I asked God why. Until recently, I never found the answer to that question.

I felt that there was no one I could really trust to always be on my side. Because of this, I withdrew from my parents and my friends. Instead, I concentrated on school and sports. Before my father got divorced, I had C's in school and played no sports. After my father got remarried, I became a straight A student and an all-star soccer player. Yet this did not make up for the parents I had lost.

At twelve years old, I never talked to my parents, except when I went into the kitchen to get something to eat. I thought everything was fine, but later I realized it wasn't. Because of all the things that had happened to me, I had isolated myself.

A day after I realized this, I called my dad at work, something I had never done before, and asked him if he could come home and talk. So he left work early and took me out to dinner. I told him how I felt and what made me feel that way. He just sat and listened. To me, that was one of the best nights of my life.

After my father and I had this talk, we started doing a lot of things together. We became father and son and developed an extremely close relationship. Three years later, we were best friends. I learned to tell my dad anything, and he always helped me with my problems. He even helped me make peace with my new stepmother. I don't think any of this would have happened, however, if I had not asked him to talk that one night long ago.

I am now fifteen years old and no longer the devastated child I once was. The divorce helped me pull my life together and form a great relationship with my father. Sometimes I think about what would have happened if my parents had never gotten divorced. I think of how I would still be lazy at school, come home, and lay on the couch. I think of how I would never have met the man I love the most, my father. Now I no longer need to ask God why. I am a much stronger person now. I love my mother very much, and I always will, but I can honestly say that I think the divorce helped me get to where I am today.

M. Kate Callaghan
Country Day School
of the Sacred Heart
Bryn Mawr, Pennsylvania

The Eleventh Rose

Whenever I reveal that I am one of ten children, I always receive an emphatic response. People either reply with smiles and admiration, "Wow!" or they produce a series of strange looks, understanding nods, and sarcastic smirks. Whatever type of feedback I receive doesn't change my great appreciation for every member of my family; at least it doesn't anymore.

Falling second in our line of ten, I have lived most of my life experiencing people's varied views of our increasing family. While growing up, I never thought there was anything particularly extraordinary about having a big family. My parents have always instilled the belief in us that it is a blessing to have so many siblings. In fact, the words most discouraged in our family are *hate* and *shut up*, words that can prove damaging to one another. It wasn't until I ventured into my awkward adolescent years that I ever felt ashamed of the size of my family.

I began to feel this way because I was starting to understand some of the things people were saying and just how demeaning they were. Some members of my mother's family would indicate what a waste of her education it was for her to be tied down with ten kids. I was repeatedly brought to tears by ignorant comments made about my parents' sex life by the puberty-stricken boys in my class. Minor incidents, such as people walking past our fifteen-seat van, stopping to point at each one of us and mouthing the numbers as if they were counting creatures in a circus sideshow made me feel self-conscious and confused. Were we strange? It wasn't any single occurrence, but an accumulation of many, that gave rise to these new feelings of shame.

This past summer, the situation worsened. My siblings and I are all approximately a year and a half apart in age. During the summer the youngest turned eighteen months old. Almost immediately I was bombarded with questions concerning whether or not my mother was pregnant. These questions persisted, and I continued to answer in the negative. My shame was quickly transformed into frustration that became increasingly potent.

Then everything turned upside down. One day this fall when I returned home from school, my five-year-old sister ran up to me saying, "Mom was going to have a baby in her stomach, but it died." She repeated it a dozen more times, but once was enough.

I went to my mother immediately, and she confirmed what my sister had said. She had been three months pregnant and had miscarried. She had had an operation that day. I walked out and burst into tears. For the remainder of the week I couldn't remove it from my mind. When people asked if my mother was pregnant, I wanted to scream at them "Not anymore!" I cried all the time, and it was seldom that I saw my mother without the trace of tears in her sad eyes.

The day my mother had the operation was a cold day in the beginning of October. That day a rose bloomed on our rose bush, the only rose that had bloomed all year.

Konstantine Karloutsos
Immaculate High School
Danbury, Connecticut

My Cousin's Courage

My cousin Maria Karloutsos is an exceptional person who continues to be an example for me. Whenever I find things difficult or unfair, I think of my cousin Maria. Then I ask myself, "What is fair?"

Is it fair when a seventeen-year-old dies in a car accident? Is it fair when a young mother dies of cancer? Is it fair that children face diseases that make them crippled? Then I think of my cousin Maria. Is it fair that she was born with the disease known as thalassemia? Of course, when you're young, you don't think about tragedies, sicknesses, or diseases unless they affect you personally.

I remember the first time I saw Maria inject a needle into her abdomen. Attached to the needle was a long hose that was connected to a syringe. The syringe was placed in a pump that slowly injected the medication called desphoral into her body. This pump and syringe are placed in a small cloth sack that Maria puts over her shoulder. She must carry this for twelve hours a day, every day of her life! This helps keep Maria alive.

Thalassemia is a genetic blood disorder that mostly affects people from Mediterranean areas. The red blood cells produced in the bone marrow lack the ability to carry nutrients and oxygen to the body. The only way for a child to survive to adulthood is to receive blood transfusions. From the age of six months, Maria began to receive blood transfusions every three weeks. She had to go to the Children's Hospital in Boston where they would first take blood tests. Then she would be infused with new blood, a process that usually took many hours.

Thankfully, scientists developed the desphoral treatment that cleanses the body and its organs of most of the dead red blood cells that have built up. Thalassemia usually causes people to die between the ages of twenty and thirty. We're hoping and praying that with this treatment Maria will live beyond her thirties, forties, and fifties.

When you're with Maria you know that you're alive. Life is filled with joy. When you're with Maria you feel the enthusiasm of life, and you always want to be a part of it. I am amazed at how this tough little woman can bring happiness to others.

Despite the struggles, the fears, the hardship, the many difficulties, Maria lives her life to its fullest. Although moments of despair may come, she never allows them to interfere with life. Last year Maria graduated from Boston College with a degree in teaching. She wants to teach.

Many times I have heard my cousin say, "I do not allow my illness to negatively affect my life. Many times I must compensate and try harder to keep my life active and normal. Sometimes it's difficult to be a doer, rather than a quitter, but because I love people and being involved in many activities, I try to remain patient and confident!"

Seeing my cousin and thinking about her at those challenging times in my life gives me the desire to not give up. Like Maria, I want to face life with courage, always be motivated, and never give up. Though this disease is life threatening, my cousin chooses not to be defeated by it. She is a beautiful, intelligent, caring, and loving cousin to me, and a great inspiration. Most importantly, she has accelerated my motivation to "never give up!"

Name Withheld
Lancaster Catholic High
School
Lancaster, Pennsylvania

Depression

What is the cause of my depression? Why am I suffering from it? Does anyone understand what I'm going through? Do people think less of me because I am depressed and have been in the hospital for treatment? These are a few of the many questions I have been tossing around in my head. Depression is the hardest thing I have ever had to face, and believe me, I did not want to face it.

There are eleven symptoms of depression. To some degree, I had all of them. I experienced persistent sad and empty moods. I had a slight loss of interest in school (I wasn't sure if this was caused by my depression or senioritis). I was always tired. I lost my appetite; I rarely ate a decent meal. I had a hard time making simple decisions and remembering little things. I felt guilty about everything, things that I now know had nothing to do with me. I snapped at everyone. It seemed like I never stopped crying, and I had a never-ending headache. But the most potentially damaging symptom was suicidal thoughts.

I thought about death and suicide daily. At first I thought mainly about dying, not killing myself. I would pray to God to take me in my sleep. I'm not sure I really wanted to die; I just wanted to be happy, and the best place I knew of to be happy was heaven.

Soon I began to think of ways to kill myself. I thought that my life was worthless, and that if I died people would grieve for a while, but then they would get on with life and forget all about me.

One day I couldn't get myself out of bed, so I stayed home and thought all day. I thought about death and my worthless life, and I attempted suicide. I tried to suffocate myself. I stopped myself before any physical damage was done, but I was emotionally distraught.

The next day, when I went to see my therapist, I told her what I had done and how I had felt. She asked me to promise her that I wouldn't hurt myself before talking to either her or my mom about it. I couldn't. I wanted to, but I didn't think it was a promise I could keep. So she told me I should go to the hospital that afternoon. She said that I was too much of a threat to myself.

Being in the hospital for four days was the best thing I could have done for myself. It was also the hardest. I never thought that at the age of seventeen I would be signing myself into a mental health care unit. Being in there made me see everything I had to live for. I saw how many people loved me and missed me when I was only gone for four days.

I am much closer to my friends and family now. I talked with my parents about the bad aspects of our family relationship, and things are much better. My parents are trying very hard. Everyone has been very supportive of me. I don't want to die anymore, and I rarely think about suicide. I am not completely recovered, but I'm on my way.

Admitting that I needed help was the hardest step. With that conquered, I know that I can tackle anything, even if I do need help sometimes. I have a new level of self-confidence that I thoroughly enjoy. I am truly happy to be alive.

Parady Sok-Kim
Nerinx Hall
Webster Groves, Missouri

Coming Along

The wind was very strong that day. The pine trees howled along the west coast of France. Despite the weather, she had told me she wanted to walk a little, but I knew that she was doing it for me. Her left side was paralyzed from the stroke that she had suffered a year before when I was twelve. Her face appeared to be a pure porcelain white, in contrast to my dark, Cambodian complexion. We said good-bye to Philbée, my Papa, and slowly walked. Her hand was heavy on my arm. We had barely made three meters when she was whispering that we should go back home. I believed that the next time we would go farther. I was too young to understand that she would die within two years.

I was born in Paris in 1976 to young Cambodian refugee parents who had no knowledge of the French language and culture. My father accompanied my mother to the hospital for my birth, but when he saw that the baby was a girl, he denied his responsibility, and left my mother, Arone Sahrung, shortly thereafter. In desperation, my mother gave me up to an agency who found a retired French couple who thought they were providing fresh country air to a needy baby for three months. Instead of three months, my country vacation turned into my entire childhood.

My idyllic childhood was filled with fresh air, races with the dogs through the fields, apple picking in the fall with Papa, sneaking into Maman's apron in the kitchen while she made jelly from the fruit we picked. We lived in an old remodeled farmhouse about an hour and a half from Paris. How funny we must have seemed to other drivers on our way to our summer house in La Baule, on the French coast. Maman and Papa in their late seventies. Maman driving because Papa had become nearly blind. In the back of a small Peugeot, me playing with the two French poodles, the two parrots in the trunk. Not restrained by modesty, we loudly sang *La Vie en Rose*. Only the Siamese cat felt embarrassed by such eccentric gypsy behavior.

But my childhood ended very suddenly when Maman had her first stroke. Our life became a series of trips to clinics and hospitals. Rehabilitation, re-education without end; I felt cheated out of my mother's energy and vitality. At school in La Baule, where we had moved permanently, I was not doing well. My grades were unsatisfactory. My teachers were very pessimistic about my abilities. My report cards began to say things like "Very disquieting results" and "Why this drop? Time to react."

But at home there was much to do to care for my parents who were now in their eighties. I remember one nightmare night. My dad became extremely ill, and I went with him to the hospital. When I got home in a taxi, I found that my mother had fallen outside in the garden. She was confused and was going to buy milk. It was only the next day that I found out that she had broken ribs and needed to be hospitalized. At age thirteen, I felt humiliated to have to beg for someone to take me home for the night. Two years later Maman died. At school, my teachers treated me like a charity case. My grades continued to drop.

Meanwhile, an American couple, Bob and Barbara Kelley, acquaintances of my parents, offered me an opportunity to spend summers with them in Saint Louis and learn English. The fourth summer, when I turned seventeen, they proposed I stay and go to high school at Nerinx Hall in Webster Groves. A brand new start! But this meant starting over with a new country, a new culture, new parents, new friends, a new school, and most of all, a new language.

In France, English was a three hour a week course. In Saint Louis, it turned into eighteen hours a day! It was arduous, and I spent long hours with books and dictionaries. In school there were only two foreign students, and the other one already spoke English. It was like being handicapped. But I had a goal. I was going to go to college in America! My new parents were supportive in their sponsorship to help me achieve my goal.

In my junior year, I didn't have much time to spare to be involved with extracurricular activities. I needed many hours a day just to do my homework. Along the way I made friends. I was valued for my participation and goodwill in classes. My teachers never put me down, unlike my teachers in France. They seemed to appreciate my work and were always encouraging. I was elected to be part of the prom court. For me, this meant that I was accepted among the other students. And I achieved a B average in a school with high standards!

My life has changed, but I go back to France at Christmas and in the summer to be with Papa. Even though I'm not with him during the year, I can feel that he is proud of my long journey and success. He has always been with me each step of the way. I send him tapes since he is blind and cannot read letters. Sometimes we talk on the phone for a few minutes.

I will attend Drake University in the fall. It won't be easy, but I know I can do it. I now have confidence in myself.

She is beside me, a white-haired old lady. Her breath is heavy. She is already tired, and she indicates that she needs to sit on her bed. We went farther today, maybe she's doing better. I look out the window and the parking lot of the hospital is full today. A nurse comes. "Parady, we need you in Room B12." Another Sunday afternoon as a volunteer on the geriatric floor at Saint Joseph's Hospital.

Brooke Prudhomme
Saint Agnes Academy
Memphis, Tennessee

Christy Snyder
Mercy High School
Farmington Hills, Michigan

Mercy in Disguise

I have always participated in both summer and winter sports for enjoyment and competition. When my two brothers and I are not swimming on our summer swim team, my family spends most of the summer boating on the lake.

One Fourth of July, my parents invited several other families to our property on Lake Charlevoix. I was having a great time until my dad let my best friend's father take over the driver's seat in the boat. I was getting ready to water-ski and had just put my foot into the ski when this man started to go. Because I was not yet ready, the rope became wrapped around my knee, and I was dragged about one hundred feet before anyone realized what had happened. The rest of that summer I had to settle for watching the swim meets and tennis matches.

My knee did seem to heal. I was just fine, in fact, until this past spring. While playing soccer, my knee constantly hurt. I went to a specialist and found out I had osteo chondritis dessicans, a defect that causes the blood supply to be cut off from the bone and cartilage. The doctor said I must stop all physical activity and be put on crutches so that my knee would have a chance, hopefully, to heal. My body was between a child's and an adult's developmentally, which meant healing was questionable. If I did not follow the doctor's instructions, surgery would become a possibility.

I learned all of this on the first day of my high school's tennis team tryouts. I had played junior varsity as a freshman, and the coach had already told me that chances were good that I would make the varsity team this year. So I was badly disappointed that I would not be able to try out for the team.

Now that I had so much extra time on my hands, my mom said that I needed to get involved in something else. She suggested I resume piano lessons, but that sounded incredibly boring to me. I decided to get more involved in my church by attending our youth group's Wednesday night sessions. At first, I was not always really comfortable. After a couple of weeks, however, I began to enjoy going and playing our silly games, singing songs, and listening to the short talks applicable to a teenager's life. I even started to make some good friends at church.

Our youth group also engages in service projects and, after a few trips to the inner city, I found a great joy in serving others. I now jump—although not literally—at any and every opportunity to do service in the community, and I have far exceeded the twenty-five hours required for graduation at my school. I have even become involved in a Monday night Bible study with some of the same people from our youth group. I have come to enjoy this equally as much as I do our social and sport activities at school.

In a way, I am almost happy that I injured my knee, for it has given me time for spiritual growth. Not only am I closer to God now, but I am closer to a more diverse group of people than I would otherwise have been. I have also made some very close friends in the process.

Now that my knee is healing, I am gradually getting back into sports, and I am playing on Mercy's soccer team. My priorities are different, however. Sports now come second, and if a conflict ever arises between soccer and one of our service projects, I am sure the soccer team will manage quite well without me!

Name Withheld
Trinity High School
River Forest, Illinois

Accidental Closeness

When my father was in a car accident in January, he lost his whole memory. He did not know who his family was, what his name was, or where he was. It was very hard for me to go to the hospital every day to visit him. Many times I would just sit outside his room and cry because I could not handle it. I took this whole thing worse than the others in my family. I was very close to my father, and it hurt me very much to see him that way.

The thing that bothered me the most was that he had no memories of us together. It seemed like he lived his whole life for nothing. I kept wondering why God would let this happen to someone who was trying to help someone else. It seemed like the whole world was coming to an end and nothing would get better.

Before my father was in this accident, my family fought a lot. My mother and father were constantly arguing. I was always in an argument with him, and my sister and I fought too. After this tragedy, we had to get along in order to comfort and be there for one another. I prayed every night that my father would get better. Even though I was upset about every-thing, I thanked God that nothing else happened to him. He could have been killed, or lost his speech or sight.

After being in the hospital for a month, my father came home. This was very hard for him and for my whole family. He was scared because he could not remember us or the house. We had to show him where everything was and what was his.

I was hurt because he would not talk to me. I wanted my father back. During this whole incident, I never lost faith in God. I prayed and prayed that he would remember. Every day my dad went to a rehabilitation center where they worked with his mind. After going for two weeks, he started having flashbacks of when I was little, when he met my mom, and of the accidents he had seen while working on the highway. He told me he did not like to have those bad flashbacks because they would depress and upset him. Even so, these few memories made me happy. As time passed, his old personality and habits started coming back. Even though these things had annoyed me before, my attitude had changed.

Though I was close to my father before, I became closer after all of this. When he came home from the hospital, my mom told him that I thought he did not love me anymore because he never talked to me. While I was eating breakfast before leaving for school one day, my father told me that I was his favorite and that he loved me very much. I'll never forget that day as long as I live. I could not help crying because it gave me such a good feeling inside.

Although my father's accident was tragic, it brought my family closer together. And even though I could not understand why God would let this happen, I now know that he lets things happen for a reason.

Maureen McLaughlin
Holy Names Academy
Seattle, Washington

My Horse, My World

To many people, horses are just animals that require food and exercise; yet to some, horses reflect the beauty and complexity of nature. I was brought into this world a horse lover. As a young child, I would build stables and cut out toy horse blankets with each horse's name carefully written on the sides. I can remember making my parents stop the car so I could stare with intense wonder and excitement at a horse. It was not until I turned thirteen, however, that my passion became my life.

I had saved up every penny that I had earned, and I was finally ready to purchase the horse of my dreams. Banjo was a four-year-old Appaloosa thoroughbred gelding. I can recall peering into his stall after I received the official bill of sale and, with tears in my eyes, I repeated, "You are mine, you are my very own horse!"

Banjo and I shared many wonderful times together. During the winter months I would ride him in the lighted indoor arena after school, and I would sink my hands into his long winter coat to keep them warm. The summer provided endless hours of trail rides, shows, baths, and simply grazing in the grass under the warm sun. Every waking moment was spent at the stables with Banjo and my friends.

When asked why I devoted so much of my time to horses, the only explanation that I could give was that I loved them, an answer that can be understood only by truly devoted horse lovers. Banjo was my responsibility, my hobby, my pet, my friend, my everything. He would always listen as I rambled on about my boyfriends, school, and family life. He was always willing to be hugged as I cried, and he never failed to lick my face or give a consoling nicker.

Then last December I felt as though my world was coming to an end. At an earlier horse show, Banjo had hurt his leg. At first the injury appeared to be minor, but after six months of stall rest and over a thousand dollars' worth of tests, the prognosis was not good. The vet informed me that the injury to his ligament was permanent, and that if I were to try to ride him at his previous level, he would eventually become completely crippled. The vet thought that I should think about having him put to sleep unless I could find him a home in which he would receive excellent care and only very light, gentle exercise.

Words could not describe the way that I felt inside; he was my horse, my world. I was torn because, confined to his stall, Banjo was miserable, yet he was too young and lively to be put down. The grim fate of my horse seemed inevitable.

I had just about given up hope when I received a call from Little Bits Therapeutic Riding Center. One of the instructors wanted to see if Banjo might work in their handicapped riders' program. Banjo was a hit! He obeyed their commands, and they determined him to be in good health. A few days later, I trailered Banjo to Little Bits, where he received training and was put into the program.

I work as a volunteer at Little Bits every weekend, where I am able to see Banjo and give him a week's worth of love. He continues to be a success in the program. I am reminded of the joy that he gave me for so many years when I see the children's faces light up as he whinnies to them. I am confident that Banjo will continue to reflect the beauty and grace of the equine species, as well as demonstrate a horse's ability to give love to those who need it most.

The Seventh Grade

Colleen Young
Academy of the Holy Names
Albany, New York

I was twelve years old. Seventh grade was quickly approaching, and I looked forward to it with much anticipation. It was going to be a year of first crushes, middle school dances, and slumber parties. Or so I thought.

When the first day arrived, I walked into the classroom with a new purple backpack and perfectly curled hair. After all, first impressions in the seventh grade are everything. The room was filled with excitement while everyone shared their news of the summer. Mrs. Farrell was going to have a baby. Jason got his braces off. Jenny had gone to an island with her family for two weeks and had the seashells to prove it.

Of course we all knew of the situation in the Middle East. We understood that there was a bad guy named Hussein and that Americans were being sent to Kuwait to fight his army. Kristy even knew where Iraq was on the classroom map. That was about as much as we could or wanted to understand. After all, world news was grown-up stuff, and we had more important matters, like the seventh grade, to think about.

Mrs. Bambrick decided we should each write a letter to an unknown soldier. She would then mail them to Kuwait as part of a community effort. We could deal with that. It was only one letter, and it wouldn't interfere with Louisa's sleepover on Friday.

Three weeks passed. We began to hear more of the situation in the Middle East. Our parents stared for hours at CNN, their minds consumed with the potential war, as we completed weekly spelling units and pre-algebra.

Unexpectedly, I received a letter from the soldier to whom I had written. Suddenly I was thrown into an unreal world, so far away. His name was Steven, and he lived in California. I read his letter to the class that afternoon.

"Colleen, hi, I'm the soldier that got your letter. I've been in the army for three years now. I have one more to go. I came into the army so they would pay for my college. . . ."

It was inconceivable! My sister was in college! I was corresponding with a soldier halfway around the world! All of a sudden I understood my parents' daily concerns. In those few minutes my life changed incredibly. The Gulf crisis became my only thought. To think, I had been worried about whether Mr. Collins had seen me passing notes in history while a man in Kuwait was worrying about whether he would be alive the next day!

As Desert Shield became Desert Storm, our correspondence continued. A relationship developed between my soldier and me. We became friends, sharing opinions on music and sports. My birthday was coming soon. However, it wasn't colored balloons that decorated my front lawn, but yellow ribbons. I had placed them around each tree, as high as I could reach, as a symbol of hope that Steven would soon be home. I often refused invitations to slumber parties and dances because I wanted the time to write to my soldier.

After several long months, the forces began taking action, although Steven was one of the last to be sent in: "Still no fighting with the ground forces. If they're not going to use us, I wish they would let us go home, but it's not going to happen. It's been six months that I've been here. . . ."

As time passed, his tone became more anxious and distressed. The letters that once said "when I come home" had altered to "if I come home." I was faced with the possibility that he may never come home. It was an ongoing nightmare. History had become reality.

Steven didn't get killed in the Gulf War. After too many torturous months, my soldier returned home. A Christmas had come and gone; it was a new year. With all of these changes, I too was drastically changed. I was nothing like the seventh grader I had envisioned. I had become very involved in a war, and aware of how precious a life could be.

One afternoon, after a long, scary pause in Steven's letters, I received a phone call. It was Steven. "I'm home," he began.

Ben Mercer
Holy Cross High School
Louisville, Kentucky

J. J. Mammi
Roanoke Catholic School
Roanoke, Virginia

A Foster Child

A few years ago, my family and I received our first foster child. His name was Charlie, and he and I were the best of enemies and total rivals for the next two years. All the time it was "who is stronger, who's taller, who's smarter," etc. Those two years were the longest of my life. Countless times I begged my parents to ask the agency to take him back, but they always said that caring for him was what God wanted us to do.

Last December, we got a 16-year-old girl who was recovering from anorexia. We went to meet her at Saint Alban's Psychiatric Center. She seemed nice and agreeable. But, then again, they all do for the first couple of weeks, until they've confirmed the stability of their place in your home. Then they unleash their evils, first to the siblings, and then to the parents.

On the next Sunday we took her to Mass, although she was Baptist, because she wanted to see how we worshiped. Then we went to a Christmas concert at Saint Andrew's.

About three months later, we found out that she smoked and had been since she was ten. After that she seemed to unfold her true self faster than we could keep up. After a few more months, we decided that it was time for her to leave.

A couple of times I wanted to give some of the foster kids a sock in the jaw, but I held back and tried to talk my way out of it. I even managed to hold my tongue and not give them any insults they would remember. And even though lots of times were bad, *all* weren't bad. There were times when we would laugh and play games, watch movies, and have fun.

Over the course of the past five years, we have had nine foster children ranging in age from seven to eighteen. And even though, while they were here, I never would have admitted it, I learned a lot from their residence. I learned that there are kids right by us who don't have loving parents to go home to. It has also helped me to realize how many blessings I have. It has helped my family to weave a tighter web in that we give more love to each other. There is no lack of love in our house.

Christine Ervin
Divine Child High School
Dearborn, Michigan

Georgetown's Words

As I waded through the customers on my way into the actual kitchen part of the Manna Meals Soup Kitchen in downtown Detroit, I struggled to maintain my frozen smile while fearing the experience to come. Many say that homeless people shouldn't be feared, but their way of life is foreign to me. I am helplessly ignorant. And ignorance is fear, so in retrospective rationalization, I was right to fear them. Wasn't I?

Broken bottles lined the stairway entrance to the dirt-stained dining area. Arranged in a somewhat methodical manner, the tables made the room look like it had been abandoned after a series of intense Bingo games. Nothing made the place appealing. Although ugliness and depression loomed like storm clouds, I knew that somewhere amidst all this coldness must lie a sense of hope and peace.

Hope hid suppressed in the sunken eyes of the homeless men and women. After years of struggle, the pleasant dreams of life-to-be had slipped away, hard to hold on to. One man, who'll be referred to as Georgetown (due to his Georgetown University apparel), changed my dismal view of these broken people. He shared some of himself with me by helping me to see that the door of hope cracked open for some.

Georgetown looked at me and said, "You're gonna make it, kid. Somehow, something went wrong, and I didn't make it. I'm thirty-three years old, but I'm not giving up. I keep praying to the Lord, and I know it will all work out. You keep praying too, and he'll help us both make something of ourselves."

My eyes filled with tears at the sincerity of his manner and at the apparent faith he possessed. Georgetown turned my whole attitude around. Suddenly the room seemed different: warmly inviting to the troubled souls of both the homeless and the volunteer. It became clear that we all share in the same struggle to understand each other and accept the lifestyles we live.

Georgetown guided me to sense the peace, both in myself and in those around me. I began to appreciate the things I have, and to admire those people who cope with having less. That day, I learned about misled presumptions and I again witnessed the awesome power of God. God brought light into a dark atmosphere and showed his kind presence amidst a world of cruelty. Everyone who visited the soup kitchen that day received food: the customers, physically, and the volunteers, spiritually.

Brooke Bell
Saint Pius X Catholic
High School
Atlanta, Georgia

New Faith

My father is the most incredible man. I am sure most people can say or would like to say that about their father, but to me, even the word *incredible* cannot sum up this person. He is loving, thoughtful, hardworking, handsome, and successful. He is stubborn and confident, but most of all, my father is blessed.

I almost lost my father in a serious and quite baffling accident. One Sunday afternoon my father was on the golf course, when a large tree fell on top of him, crushing him and the golf cart he was driving. The tree that was pinning him was eventually moved with the help of many neighbors. He was taken to the intensive care unit of North Fulton Hospital in critical condition. He had lost an excessive amount of blood, broken his arm, and seriously damaged his left leg.

At first, my two sisters and I were unsure of the serious-ness of the injuries and feared for my father's life. My mother spent night and day at the hospital. A few days after the acci-dent, the doctor informed us that my father's leg had to be amputated at mid-thigh. His leg would not fully recover, and there was no alternative.

After the surgery, he remained in ICU for one month and then went to rehab for a few weeks. I think this was the most difficult time for my family. Even though we were thankful that death had passed him by, watching his struggle to recover was heartbreaking.

My father was always determined. You could see that look in his face every time he lifted a weight with his arms or raced around in his wheelchair. People would come to visit and couldn't believe him. He was positive and always had a smile on his face. We called him Super Dad!

Dad soon came home. We were all happy, but it was a big adjustment. He needed constant care and attention. I still remember that period of confusion and feeling uncomfortable. It was hard to see a man who used to go hang gliding and motorcycle riding on his Harley Davidson, lying helplessly on the couch. One thing is for sure, I have never loved my father so much. I thank God every night for saving his life.

A few months later, he got a prosthetic leg. We were all excited that he would be able to walk again. My father had the leg only a few days before I left for France for a month. I was afraid to leave because I was unsure of what to expect when I returned. Needless to say, I wasn't disappointed. The night I returned, I was greeted by my father at the airport, practically racing me to the baggage claim. He walked almost perfectly and was very proud of it.

Almost a year later, my father returned to work. He strums his classical guitar incessantly and has even played golf several times. It has been hard for my father and my family, but I firmly believe that all the love and support and, most importantly, my father's ambitions account for his recovery.

I have found a new faith in God and a new appreciation for life. The best part is that my school, our neighbors, and our friends all prayed daily for my father, and he still, to this day, attributes his recovery to all their prayers.

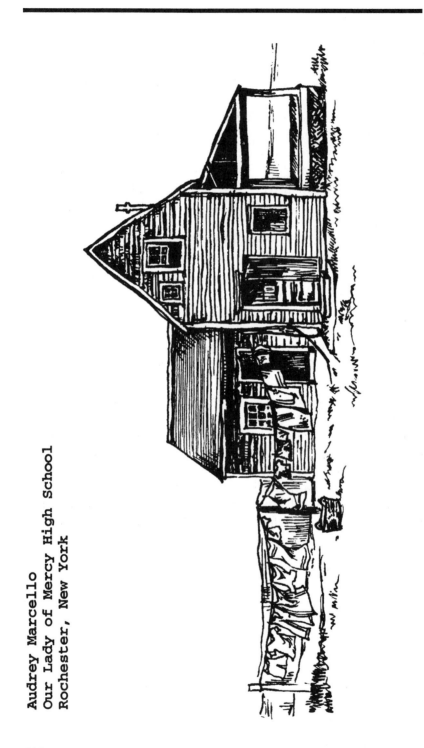

Audrey Marcello
Our Lady of Mercy High School
Rochester, New York

Index by School

Gonzaga Preparatory School
Spokane, WA
Claudia Rubio   cover

Holy Cross High School
Louisville, KY
Ben Mercer   115
Shawn M. Beirne   71
Mandy Rager   37
Amy Westerman   91

Holy Names Academy
Seattle, WA
Maureen McLaughlin   110

Immaculate High School
Danbury, CT
Ann Marie Hines   56
Name Withheld   38
Konstantine Karloutsos   98

Lancaster Catholic High School
Lancaster, PA
Name Withheld   100

LaSalle High School
Pasadena, CA
Name Withheld   94

Main Catholic High School
San Rafael, CA
Megan Keane   50

Mercy High School
Farmington Hills, MI
Christy Snyder   106

Mercyhurst Preparatory School
Erie, PA
Shannon Anderson   92

Mount de Sales Academy
Macon, GA
Name Withheld   64

Nerinx Hall
Webster Groves, MO
Parady Sok-Kim   102

Notre Dame Academy
Toledo, OH
Allison Hawkins   43

O'Hara High School
Kansas City, MO
Matt Kruger   68

Our Lady of Mercy High School
Rochester, NY
Audrey Marcello   122

Reicher High School
Waco, TX
Name Withheld   88

Roanoke Catholic School
Roanoke, VA
J. J. Mammi   116

Sacred Heart Catholic School
Morrilton, AR
Name Withheld   28

Saint Agnes Academy
Memphis, TN
Cissy Paig   15
Joanna D'Gerolamo   25
Amy Brookshire   85
Brooke Prudhomme   105

Saint Bernard High School
Fitchburg, MA
Name Withheld   26

Saint Catherine Indian School
Santa Fe, NM
Name Withheld   74

Saint Dominic Regional High School
Lewistown, ME
Name Withheld   19

Saint Frances Academy
Baltimore, MD
Name Withheld   46

Saint Francis Borgia Regional High School
Washington, MO
Teresa Ann Clancy   34

Saint Mark's High School
Wilmington, DE
Michael Over   32

Saint Mary's High School
Sleepy Eye, MN
Name Withheld   66

Saint Peter's Prep
Jersey City, NJ
Anthony Vitanzo   86

Saint Pius X Catholic High School
Atlanta, GA
Brooke Bell   120

Saint Raymond Academy for Girls
Bronx, NY
Name Withheld   16

Saint Scholastica High School
Chicago, IL
Name Withheld   76
Mai Tran   58
Natasha Achanzar   54

Stella Maris High School
Rockaway Park, NY
Name Withheld   52

Trinity High School
River Forest, IL
Name Withheld   108

Villa Joseph Marie High School
Holland, PA
AnnElise Collier   72
Name Withheld   22

Villa Walsh Academy
Morristown, NJ
Tatiana Kazdoba   40

Index by Theme